ANTHRO

GUIDELINES

RUDOLF STEINER

TRANSLATED BY FRANK THOMAS SMITH

ANTHROPOSOPHICAL PUBLICATIONS

Anthroposophical Guidelines

Copyright © 2017 by Frank Thomas Smith.

Cover design by James D. Stewart

Edited by James D. Stewart

This volume contains a collection of short essays by Steiner for the members of the Anthroposophical Society. They were written near the end of Steiner's life and in a way summarize, in highly concentrated form, the whole of anthroposophy. Each essay ends with a short summary of its contents and these are known as the "leading thoughts." The leading thoughts are mantras and can be used quite fruitfully for meditation.

Translated by
Frank Thomas Smith
Visit his website at https://SouthernCrossReview.org/

Printed in the United States of America

First Printing: Aug 2022

Anthroposophical Publications
https://AnthroposophicalPublications.org/

ISBN-13: 978-1-948302-41-8 Paperback
978-1-948302-46-3 eBook

Table of Contents

Anthroposophical Guidelines 1

On the Anthroposophical Guidelines.....................................1

On the preceding Guidelines about the............................11

image-nature of man 11

On Understanding Spirit and Experiencing Destiny 19

Spiritual Realms and Human Self-knowledge 23

At the Dawn of the Michael Age 31

The State of the Human Soul before the Michael Age..........35

Aphorisms 39

The Pre-Michaelic and the Michaelic Path..........................45

Michael's Task in the Sphere of Ahriman 49

Michael's Experiences during the Fulfillment of his Cosmic
    Mission 53

The Future of Humanity and Michael's Activity 57

Humanity's Michael-Christ-Experience 61

Michael's Mission in the Cosmic Age of Human Freedom......65

The Cosmic Thoughts in Michael's Activity and in Ahriman's.71

First Contemplation: How Michael prepares his earthly mission
    in the spiritual world by conquering Lucifer at the Gates of
    the Consciousness Soul..77

Second Contemplation: How the Michael Forces functioned
    during the first unfolding of the Consciousness Soul 85

Continuation of the Second Contemplation: Hindrance and
    Furtherance of the Michael Forces at the Dawn of the
    Conscious Soul Age 91

Third Contemplation: Michael's anxiety about human evolution
    before the time of his earthly activity..........................97

Christmas Contemplation: The Logos Mystery.................. 103

Additional Guidelines relating to the foregoing Christmas
    Contemplation 108

Heavenly History — Mythological History; Earthly History — The
    Mystery of Golgotha 111

What is Revealed when One Looks Back at Repeated Earth Lives 119

What is Revealed when between Death and a New Birth, One Looks Back into Previous Lives — Part 1 123

What is Revealed when between Death and a New Birth, One Looks Back into Previous Lives — Part 2 127

What is the Reality of the Earth within the Macrocosm? 133

Sleeping and Waking in Light of the preceding Contemplations 137

Gnosis and Anthroposophy 141

Human Freedom and the Age of Michael 145

Man as a Thinking and Remembering Being 149

The Macrocosmic Nature of Man 153

The Sensing and Thinking Organization of Humanity in Relation to the World 159

Memory and Conscience 163

The Supposed Extinguishing of Spiritual Knowledge in Modern Times 167

The Historical Turbulence at the Dawning of the Consciousness Soul 171

From Nature to Sub-Nature 175

About The Translator 179

On-Line Activities 181

Other Books 183

Anthroposophical Guidelines

by Rudolf Steiner

*These Guidelines were written from February 1924
through March 1925 for members of the
Anthroposophical Society*

On the Anthroposophical Guidelines

1. Anthroposophy is a path of knowledge which would guide the spiritual in the human being to the spiritual in the cosmos. It manifests as a necessity of the heart and feeling. It must find its justification in being able to satisfy this need. Only those who find in anthroposophy what they seek in this respect can appreciate it. Therefore only those who feel certain questions about the nature of man and the world as basic necessities of life, like hunger and thirst, can be anthroposophists.

2. Anthroposophy imparts knowledge obtained by spiritual means. Yet it only does this because everyday life and a science dependent only upon sense perception and intellectual activity lead to a boundary where the human being's soul must wither if it cannot cross. This everyday life and this science do not lead to the boundary in a way that one is prevented from crossing it; rather at this boundary of sense perception the view of the spiritual world is revealed by the soul itself.

3. Some people think that *all* insights end at the boundaries of sense perception. If they were attentive to *how* they become conscious of these boundaries, they would also find in this very consciousness the capacity to transcend these boundaries. A fish swims to the boundaries of water; it must go back because it lacks the physical organs to live out of water. Man arrives at the boundaries of sense perception; he can realize that on the way

1

there sufficient strength of soul has been acquired to live in the elements which are not limited by sense perception.

4. Man requires knowledge of the spiritual world for security in his feelings and for the healthy development of his will. Then he can sense to a large extent the greatness, beauty and wisdom of the natural world. The latter does not, however, answer the questions about his own being. This being holds the matter and forces of the natural world together in the living human bodily form only until the person crosses the threshold of death. At that point nature takes over the form. It cannot hold it together, only tear it apart. Great, beautiful, wisdom-filled Nature may answer the question of how the human form disintegrates, but not how it is held together. No theoretical objection can erase *this* question from the sensitive human soul if it does not wish to deceive itself. Its presence must ceaselessly maintain the desire for spiritual paths to knowledge of the cosmos in every human soul which is truly awake.

5. The human being needs spiritual self-knowledge for inner peace. He finds himself in his thinking, feeling and willing. He sees how thinking, feeling and willing are dependent upon the natural human being. Where health and illness are concerned, they must follow the physical body in its strength and debilitation. Sleep extinguishes them. Life's experiences show how dependent spiritual experience is on the physical body. One may therefore come to the conclusion that self-knowledge is lost amidst these everyday experiences. Then the essential question arises: whether self-knowledge and therewith certainty about the true self, beyond ordinary experience, is even possible. Anthroposophy wishes to answer this question based upon sound spiritual experience. It is not based on mere opinion or belief, but on experience of the spirit, which is as certain as the experience of the body.

6. When we look at lifeless nature we find a world revealed in coherent relationships. We Investigate these relationships and find that they are the functions of natural laws. But we also find that through these laws lifeless nature unites with the earth as a

whole. From this unification of the lifeless with the earth, we can then proceed to a contemplation of the plant-world. We see how the cosmos beyond the earth sends the forces from outer space which extracts life from the lap of the lifeless. We become aware of the essence in the living which extracts from the mere earthly and manifests what works down upon the earth from the distance of cosmic space. In the most insignificant plant we become aware of the essence of the cosmic light beyond the earth, just as a luminous object is reflected in the eye. By such enhanced contemplation we can observe the difference between the earthly/physical, which governs the lifeless, and the outer-earthly/etheric, which acts in living things.

7. We find man as an ensouled spiritual being placed in this earthly and outer-earthly world. As long as he is in the earthly element, which contains the lifeless, he carries his physical body with him; when he develops the forces which insert the living from the cosmos into the earthly, he has an *etheric* or life-body. This contrast between the earthly and the etheric has been completely overlooked by modern thinking. For this reason, the most irrational views about the etheric have ensued. Fear of losing one's self in the fantastic has prevented discussion of this contrast. Without consideration of this contrast, however, no insight into Man and World is possible.

8. One can contemplate the nature of man insofar as it is revealed by his physical and his etheric body. We find, however, that whatever is revealed from these sources does not lead to consciousness, but remains in the unconscious. Consciousness is not illuminated, but darkened when the physical and etheric bodies' activity is increased. Even fainting spells can be the result of such increases in activity. Through such observations we realize that something is active in the human organization — and in animals as well — which is *not* the same as what is active in the physical and etheric. It is *not* active when the physical and the etheric elements are active through their own forces, but when these *cease* their activity. We arrive thus at the concept of the astral body.

9. The *reality* of the astral body is found when we advance from meditation by the thinking which is stimulated from without to inner contemplation. For this one must inwardly seize the thinking stimulated from without and intensively *experience* it in the soul as such, without relation to the outer world; and then, by means of the soul-strength acquired by this seizing and experiencing, become aware of the fact that inner organs of perception exist, which spiritually *see,* there, where the animal and human physical and the etheric bodies are bounded, in order that consciousness can arise.

10. Consciousness does *not* arise through a continuation of those activities which derive from the physical and etheric bodies; rather both of these bodies must reach rock-bottom, or even below that, in order to "make room" for consciousness. They are not the originators of consciousness, but merely provide the platform on which the spirit must stand in order to generate consciousness in earthly life. Just as man on earth needs a platform on which to stand, the spirit needs the material foundation of earth on which it can evolve. However, as a planet in space does not need a ground under it in order to claim its place, so the spirit — whose contemplation is not directed through the senses towards the material, but by its own forces towards the spiritual — does *not* need this material foundation in order to trigger its conscious activity.

11. Self-consciousness, which summarizes itself in the "I", alights from consciousness. This happens when the physical and etheric bodies are deconstructed by their own forces, thereby allowing the emergence of the spiritual in man. The deconstruction of these bodies creates the ground on which consciousness is born. Reconstruction must follow, however, if the organism is not to be destroyed. Therefore, if for the experience of consciousness deconstruction takes place, the deconstructed must be reconstructed. Self-consciousness lies in the perception of this construction. One can follow this process by interior vision. One can sense how the conscious is transformed into the self-conscious in that one creates from *one's self* an afterimage of the merely conscious. The consciousness possesses its own image in

4

the organism vacated, as it were, through deconstruction. It becomes self-consciousness when the emptiness is re-filled from within. The being capable of this fulfillment is experienced as "I".

12. The reality of the "I" is found when inner contemplation — by means of which the astral body is cognitively grasped — is developed further and living thinking is permeated with the will in meditation. At first one has devoted one's self will-less to this thinking. Thereby one has allowed a spiritual element to enter into this thinking, just as color and sound enter the eye and the ear when perceived by the senses. In this way, what one has passively been able to bring to life in consciousness can be recreated by an act of will, and in this act of will the perception of one's own "I" is enabled.

13. By means of meditation, one can find the "I" that emerges in ordinary consciousness in three additional forms: 1. In the consciousness which perceives the etheric body the "I" appears as an image — which at the same time is an active being and as such imparts shape, growth and formative forces to man. 2. In the consciousness which perceives the astral body, the "I" is manifested as a member of a spiritual world from which it derives its forces. 3. In the consciousness just described as the last to be achieved, the "I" reveals itself as an autonomous being, relatively independent of its spiritual environment.

14. The second form of the "I" that which was indicated in the thirteenth Guideline, emerges as an "image", or picture. By becoming aware of this image-nature, light is also thrown on the essence of thinking in which the "I" appears in normal consciousness. One seeks the "true I" by all kinds of reflections. But a serious insight into the experiences of this consciousness shows that one does not find the "true I" therein. What appears is rather a reflection in thought, one which is less than an image. One realizes the truth of this fact when one progresses to the "I" as an image that lives in the etheric body. And by this means one is finally urged correctly to *seek* the I as the true being of man.

15. The insight into the form in which the "I" lives in the astral body leads to a correct feeling for the relations between man and the spiritual world. This I-form is submerged in the dark depths of the unconscious for normal experience. In these depths man connects with the spiritual cosmic being through inspiration. Only an extremely weak feeling-like reflection of this inspiration, which resides in the depths of the soul and derives from the distant breadth of the spiritual world, is accessible to normal consciousness.

16. The third form of the "I" gives the insight into the autonomous being of man within a spiritual world. It stimulates the feeling that the human being's visible earthly-material nature is only the physical manifestation of what he is in reality. Thus the starting point for true self-knowledge is given. For the self which shapes man in his reality is only revealed to knowledge when he advances from the thought of the I to its image, from the image to the image's creative force, and from there to the spiritual bearers of these forces.

17. Man is a being whose life evolves in the middle of two world regions. [Most likely, "three" worlds is meant. Trans.] In the development of his physical body he is integrated in a "lower world"; with his soul he forms a "middle world", and he strives towards a "higher world" through his spiritual forces. He develops his physical body with what nature has given him; he bears his soul-being as his own contribution; he finds the spiritual forces in himself as the gifts which lead him beyond himself towards participation in a divine world.

18. The spirit is creative in these three worlds. Nature is not spiritless. One also loses knowledge of nature if one is not aware of the spirit in it. Nevertheless, one will find the spirit in nature as though sleeping. Just as sleep has its function in human life and the "I" must sleep for certain periods in order to be fully awake at others, so must the cosmic spirit sleep in "nature's realm" in order to be fully awake in another.

19. In respect to the cosmos, the soul of man is a dreamer if he doesn't pay attention to the spirit which works in him. This spirit

awakens the soul-dreams — which play out in his inner life — to participation in the cosmos, from which man's true being originates. Just as the dreamer shuts himself off from the physical environment and closes himself in his own being, so his soul must lose its connection to the World-Spirit from which it originates if he refuses to hear the wake-up call of the spirit within.

20. The correct development of man's soul-life requires that he be fully conscious of the spirit's actions within him. Many adherents of the modern scientific worldview are so caught up in their prejudices that they consider general causality to be dominant in all the world's phenomena — and if man thinks that he can be the cause of something, it is an illusion. Modern science wishes to follow observation and experience with the best of intentions. But due to the prejudice about the hidden causality of human motivation, it sins against this principle. For free acts deriving from the inner human essence is an elementary result of self-observation. It must not be denied, but be brought into harmony with insight into the general causality in natural law.

21. Non-recognition of this motivation from the spiritual core of the human being is the greatest hindrance to attainment of insight into the spiritual world. For the inclusion of one's own being in the natural scheme of things diverts attention from this being. One cannot penetrate into the spiritual world unless one grasps the spirit where it is directly revealed: in objective self-observation.

22. Self-observation establishes the beginning of spirit-observation. And it can establish the correct beginning because through correct reflection one cannot stop short at it, but must advance to further spiritual cosmic substance. Just as the human body atrophies when it does not receive physical nourishment, so does the correctly self-observing person feel his Self-atrophying if he doesn't see how the forces of an active spiritual world outside him are working into it.

23. The human being enters into the spiritual world when he passes through the portal of death and feels all that he has acquired

through the bodily senses and brain in impressions and mental content during earthly life fall away. In a comprehensive tableau he is then conscious of images of his life on earth which were retained in memory in the form of image-less thoughts; or what was unnoticed during earthly life, but which made an unconscious impression on the soul. These images grow faint after a few days until they disappear. When they are completely gone, he knows that he has also laid aside his etheric body, which he recognizes as the bearer of these images.

24. After the etheric body has been laid aside, man's astral body and his "I" remain. As long as the former is still with him, it allows consciousness to experience all the unconscious contents formed when sleeping during earthly life. The judgments which the spiritual beings of a higher world instilled in the astral body during sleep are contained in these contents which, however, are hidden from earthly consciousness. The person re-lives his earthly life — in such a way, however, that the assessment of his soul-content, of his deeds and thoughts, is determined from the viewpoint of the spirit-world. He experiences his life in reverse: first the last night, then the next to last, and so on.

25. The judging of a person's life, which is experienced in the astral body after passing through the portal of death, lasts as long as the time which passed in sleep during earthly life.

26. Only after the astral body has been laid aside, after the completion of the life judgment, does man enter into the spiritual world. Therein he stands in relation to the purely spiritual beings as he did on earth to the beings and processes of nature. In spiritual experiences, everything which was exterior to him becomes interior. He doesn't merely perceive the outer world, but he experiences it in its spirituality — which was hidden from him on earth — as his inner world.

27. Man, as he is on the earth, becomes outer-world in the spirit-realm. One looks [from there] at the human being as one looks at the stars, clouds, mountains, rivers from the earth. And *this* outer world is no less rich in content than is the appearance of the cosmos when viewed from the earth.

28. The *forces* created by man's spirit in the spiritual realm continue to be active in the formation of the earthly man, just as the *deeds* carried out in physical life continue to be active as soul-content in life after death.

29. What acts in enhanced imaginative cognition is what lives in man's psychic-spiritual interior and forms his physical body; and on this foundation human existence unfolds in the physical world. The physical body, ever and again renewing itself in its metabolism, stands from birth (or rather conception) until death before the *continuously* unfolding inner human being: the physical space-body becoming a time-body.

30. In inspired cognition, imaginative images depict what the human being experiences in the time between death and a new birth in a spiritual environment. Here is visible what man is in a cosmic context, without his physical and etheric bodies through which he lived out his earthly existence.

31. In intuitive cognition the effects of previous incarnations on the present one enter consciousness. These previous incarnations, in their further development, have erased the connection they once had with the physical world. They have become the pure spiritual core of the person and as such are active in his current life. They are also an object of the cognition that is the result of the unfolding of imagination and inspiration.

32. In the human head the physical organization is a copy of the spiritual individuality. The physical and etheric parts of the head stand as a self-contained image of the spiritual, and *alongside* them the astral and "I" parts stand as autonomous psychic-- spiritual being. Therefore, the human head represents a juxtaposition of the relatively autonomous physical and etheric on one hand, and the astral and I-organization on the other.

33. In the limbs/metabolism system, the four members of the human being are intimately interconnected. The I-organization and the astral body are *not* alongside the physical and etheric parts; they are *in* them; they vivify them, activate their growth, capacity for movement and so on. Therewith, however, the limbs/metabolism

is like an evolving seed which continually strives to become "head", and which is continually prevented from doing so during man's earthly life.

34. The rhythmic organization is in the middle. Here the I-organization and the astral body alternately unite with and separate from the physical and etheric parts. The physical facsimile of this unification-separation process is breathing and blood circulation. The inbreathing process depicts unification; the outbreathing process separation. The processes in arterial blood depict unification; the processes in venous blood separation.

35. We understand the physical human being only if we think of him as an *image* of the spiritual-psychic. By itself the physical human body is incomprehensible. But in its various members it is an image of the spiritual-psychic in various ways. The head is the most perfect, complete sense-image. Everything which comprises the metabolism-limbs-system is like an image whose form has not yet been fully realized, but is still being composed. Everything which belongs to the human rhythmic organization stands, in respect to the relationship of the spiritual-psychic to the physical, between these contrapositions.

36. Whoever contemplates the human head from this viewpoint finds help in understanding spiritual imaginations; for in the head's form imaginative forms are, so to speak, solidified to physical density.

37. In the same way one can find help understanding Inspiration by contemplating the rhythmic part of the human organization. The physical aspect of life's rhythms bears the character of Inspiration as a sense-image. In the metabolism-and limbs system one has, when one contemplates it in full action, in the development of its necessary or possible functions, a sensible-supersensible image of the purely supersensible Intuitive.

On the preceding Guidelines about the image-nature of man

It is of great importance that through Anthroposophy it should be made clear that the ideas which one obtains by the observance of nature are inadequate for the contemplation of man. The way of thinking which has taken possession of human sentiment during the last centuries of spiritual evolution sins against this challenge. One becomes used to thinking about natural laws; and by means of these laws the natural phenomena observed by the senses are explained. One then looks at the human organism and thinks that it can also be explained by applying natural laws to it.

This is like considering a picture which a painter created to be the same as the substance of the colors used, as the strength used to apply the colors to the canvas, or the method with which the colors are painted on the canvas, and similar viewpoints. But all that does not reveal what the picture manifests. Completely different principles live in what the picture manifests than can be obtained by those methods.

One must be quite clear about the fact that in the human being something also manifests itself which is not comprehensible from the point of view of natural laws. If one is able to make this idea his own in the right way, then one will be able to understand the human being *as image.* In this sense, a mineral is not image. It only manifests what the senses can directly perceive.

With images, sense observation is directed *through* what is perceived to the content, which is grasped in the spirit. This is also the case when contemplating the human being. If one contemplates man according to natural laws in the right way, one does not approach what man truly is, but only what is manifested through these laws.

One must realize that when the natural laws are applied to man it is as if one were standing before a picture and only knows — that's blue, that's red — and is incapable, though inner soul activity, of associating the blue and the red to what these colors manifest.

One must perceive something quite different when applying natural laws to a mineral substance and to a human being. From a spiritual viewpoint, in the case of the mineral it is as though one were directly touching what one sees; when applying natural laws to man it is as though one stands as apart from him as one stands apart from a picture which one does not see with the eye of the soul, but merely brushes with the fingertips.

Once one understands in contemplating man, that he is the *image* of something, then one is in the right soul-disposition to advance to what this image represents.

And the image nature of man does not manifest itself in one explicit way. A sense organ is essentially least of all an image, at most a kind of manifestation of itself like a mineral. One can come closest to the sense organs through natural laws. Just look at the wonderful organization of the human eye. One *roughly* grasps this organization by means of natural laws. And it is similar with the other sense organs, although it is not so clearly the case as with the eye. It is because the sense organs demonstrate a kind of self-containment in their forms. They are included in the organism as completed formations, and as such they impart perception of the outer world.

This is not the case with the rhythmic functions in the organism. They do not manifest themselves as something complete. A continual generation and degeneration of the organism takes place in them. If the sense organs were like the rhythmic system, man would perceive the outer world as being in a state of continuous becoming.

The sense organs manifest themselves like a picture that hangs on a wall. The rhythmic system appears before us like what happens when we contemplate the canvas and the painter in the process of creating a picture. The picture does not yet exist, but it is in the process of coming into existence. What has come into being remains, at first, existent. This contemplation has to do only with a process of becoming. In contemplating the human rhythmic system, the expiring, the deconstruction, immediately connects to the coming into being, to the construction. The rhythmic system manifests a *becoming* image.

The soul's act of dedicating itself to the observation of an object which is a finished image may be called *Imagination*. The experience which must unfold in order to grasp an image in the state of becoming is, on the other hand, *Inspiration.*

It is a different story when one contemplates the metabolism and movement system of the human organism. It is as though one were standing before an empty canvas, paint-pots and an artist who has not yet begun to paint. If one wishes to grasp the metabolic and limbs system, one must develop a capacity for observance which has as little to do with what the senses see when observing the paint pots and empty canvas as these have to do with the artist's finished picture. And the activity which the person experiences in his soul spiritually from the metabolism and [limb] movements is comparable to when observing the painter, empty canvas and paint-pots, he experiences the subsequently painted picture. *Intuition* must be at work in the soul in order to grasp the metabolic and limbs system.

It is necessary that the active members of the Anthroposophical Society concentrate in this way on the Being which is the basis of anthroposophical considerations. For not only should what is gained from anthroposophical cognition be recognized, but also how one is able to experience this knowledge.

What has been explained here will lead into the following Guidelines.

38. If one has been able to contemplate man in his *image-nature* and in his revealed spirituality in accordance with the indications given in the previous Guidelines, one stands in the spiritual world where one sees man as an active spiritual being, and also sees the psychic-moral laws in their reality. For the moral world-order appears now as the earthly likeness of an order belonging to the spiritual world. And the physical and moral world-orders bond themselves in unity.

39. The *will* comes from within man. It is completely foreign to the natural laws gained from the outer world. The sense organs' similarity to external natural objects is discernible. The will cannot yet manifest itself in their activities. The essence which is revealed in the rhythmic system is less similar to everything external. The will can intervene in this system to a certain extent. But this system is still involved with becoming and dying. The will is still bound by this.

40. The nature of the metabolism and limbs system manifests itself through matter and their processes, but the matter and the processes have nothing more to do with it than the painter and his tools have to do with the finished picture. The will can therefore directly intervene. If one grasps the spiritual human being behind the one who lives and acts according to natural laws, one finds in *him* a field in which one can become aware of the will's working. Conversely, in the field of the senses will remains a meaningless word; and whoever seeks to understand it in this field fails to recognize the true nature of the will and replaces it with something else.

41. In the previous Guideline the nature of the *human will* was described. Only by becoming aware of this nature is one in a cosmic sphere in which destiny (karma) works. As long as one only sees the laws which dominate in connection with natural things and natural facts, he remains far from the laws which apply to destiny.

42. By grasping the laws of destiny in this way, it is also apparent that this destiny cannot be realized through a single physical earthly life. As long as man lives in the same physical body, he can only carry out the moral content of his will to the extent the physical body within the physical world allows. Only when he passes through the gates of death into the spiritual world is the spiritual nature of the will able to achieve its true effect. There the good and the bad will achieve spiritual fulfillment in their corresponding results for the first time.

43. By means of this spiritual fulfillment, man configures himself between death and a new birth; in his *essence* he becomes an

image of what he *did* during his life on earth. Through this, his essence, he configures his physical life upon his return to earth. The spiritual, which affects destiny, can only carry out its task in the physical when its corresponding causation has *previously* withdrawn into the spiritual world. For what is experienced in life as destiny is not built upon the results of physical occurrences, but proceeds from the spiritual.

44. A transition to the spiritual-scientific consideration of the question of destiny should be made using examples from the life of individual persons: how the path of destiny affected the course of his life. For example, how a youthful experience, surely not carried out in full freedom by the person involved, can influence his entire later life.

45. The meaning of the fact that during the course of physical life between birth and death the good can seem unhappy and evil at least apparently happy, should be depicted. Examples in pictures are more important in discussing these things than theoretical explanations, because they better prepare for spiritual scientific considerations.

46. In cases of destiny which occur in a person's life in a way that cannot be explained by his particular present earth-life, it should be shown that such occurrences quite obviously point directly to previous lives. It should of course be clear that in expounding such things nothing obligatory is meant; rather that something is said which orients thinking towards spiritual-scientific considerations of the question of destiny.

47. Only the smallest part of the formation of man's destiny enters into ordinary consciousness; it works mostly in the unconscious. But it is just by the unveiling of the threads of destiny that it becomes clear how unconscious content can become conscious. Those who claim that the temporarily unconscious must remain in the area of the unknown, and create therewith a limit to knowledge, are completely mistaken. For every element of his destiny that a person unveils, he lifts a previously unconscious content into the realm of consciousness.

48. By such unveiling, one becomes aware that destiny is not arranged during life between birth and death; rather is one impelled, just by this question of destiny, to consider the life between death and a new birth.

49. By directing the consideration of human experience beyond one's self and towards the question of destiny, one achieves a true feeling for the relationship between the material and the spiritual worlds. By observing destiny's interplay, one is already standing in the spiritual world. For the interconnections of destiny are not at all related to materiality.

50. It is extremely important to point out how the consideration of the history of humanity is vitalized when one shows that by passing from epoch to epoch in their repeated earth lives, it is the human souls themselves which carry over the results of one historical epoch into the other.

51. One may easily object that viewing history in this way takes from it its elementary and naive elements. But this is unjust. On the contrary, it deepens the view of history because it follows it within man's innermost being. History thus becomes richer and more concrete, not poorer and abstracter. In the depiction one must only develop heart and appreciation for the living human soul, into which one thereby achieves profound insight.

52. The epochs in life between death and a new life should be considered in relation to the forming of karma. The "how" of this consideration shall be the subject of the following guidelines.

53. The unfolding of human life between death and a new birth occurs in successive stages. During several days after passing through the portals of death, the forgoing life is perceived in *images*. At the same time, this perception shows the detachment of the bearer [physical body] of this life from the human psychic-spiritual being.

54. In the time which comprises approximately one-third of the forgoing earthly life, the soul experiences the effect that life must have in the sense of an ethically just world order. During this

experience, the intention is born to form the next earthly life as compensation for the forgoing one.

55. A purely spiritual, long enduring epoch follows, during which the human soul prepares its coming earth-life in the sense of karma, together with other karmically conjoined human souls and with beings of the higher hierarchies.

56. The epoch between death and a new birth, during which the person's karma is prepared, can only be described based of the results of spiritual research. But it must always be borne in mind that reason is enlightened by this description. Reason only needs to objectively consider the essence of the reality of sense perception to realize that it also points to the spiritual, as a cadaver's form points to the life [once] inherent in it.

57. The results of spiritual science show that between death and birth man belongs to spiritual realms, just as he belongs to the three realms of nature — mineral, vegetable and animal — between birth and death.

58. The mineral kingdom is recognizable in the present form of the human being; the vegetable — etheric body — is the foundation of his becoming and growing; the animal — astral body — the impulse for the unfolding of his feeling and will. The crowning of conscious feeling and will in the *self-conscious* spirit immediately makes the relation of man to the spiritual world apparent.

59. An objective consideration of thinking shows that normal consciousness's thoughts have no existence of their own, that they only appear as mirror-images of something. But the individual feels himself *alive* in thoughts. The *thoughts* do not live; rather *he* lives *in* the thoughts. This life originates in the spiritual beings of the third hierarchy, a spiritual realm (in the sense of my *Outline of Esoteric Science*).

60. Extending this objective consideration to feelings shows that although they arise from the physical organism, they cannot originate there, and that their life includes an essence which is independent of the physical organism. Man can feel himself to be in the natural world with his physical organism. But it is just then,

when he does this with self-knowledge, that he experiences himself to be in a spiritual realm through his feelings. It is the realm of the second hierarchy.

61. As a being of will, man does not turn to his physical organism, but to the outer world. He doesn't ask when he wants to walk: "What do I feel in my feet? but what is out there as a goal I want to reach." He forgets his organism when he wills. In his will he doesn't belong to *his* nature. He belongs to the spirit-realm of the first hierarchy.

On Understanding Spirit and Experiencing Destiny

To the communications and considerations which are imparted to the members, I would like now to add something which can be appropriate for enhanced understanding of the Guidelines.

Understanding of anthroposophical knowledge can be enhanced when the human soul is continually reminded of the relation between man and world.

When a person directs his attention to the world in which he is born and dies, he is initially surrounded by a plenitude of sense impressions. He thinks about these sense impressions.

When he is conscious of the following: "I have thoughts about what my senses reveal to me about the world", he is ready for self-knowledge. He can say to himself: "I" live in my thoughts. The world gives me the opportunity to experience *myself* in thought. I find myself in my thoughts when I contemplate the world.

Continuing in this contemplation the world, he removes the world from consciousness; and the I enters into it. He ceases to think of the world; he begins to experience the self. When, conversely, he brings his attention to his inner life in which the world is mirrored, the events of his life related to destiny emerge in which the human self participates — from the point in time he can remember. He experiences his own being in the sequence of this destiny-experience.

To the extent one is conscious of this: "I have lived a destiny with my Self", he can introduce contemplation of the world. He can say to himself: "I was not alone in my destiny; the world intervened in my experience. I *wanted* this or that; the world flowed into my will. I find the world in my will in that I experience this will in self-contemplation.

Thus living into his self, this self departs from consciousness and the world enters. He ceases to experience the self; he begins to be aware of the world with his feelings.

I extend thinking out into the world; I find myself there; I submerge in my self, I find the world there. When one senses *this* strongly enough, he stands within the riddles of world and human existence.

Then to feel: "I struggle to grasp the world by thinking, but it is merely me trapped in this thinking" — which reveals the first world-riddle.

To feel in his self that he has been formed by destiny and in this forming to sense the world's happenings; this points him to the second world-riddle.

By experiencing this riddle of world and man, a state of mind germinates in which one can encounter anthroposophy in such a way that he receives an impression within that awakens his interest.

For anthroposophy maintains the following: A spiritual experience exists which does not ignore the world in thinking. One can also still *live* in thinking. It provides an inner experience in meditation in which one does not lose the sense-world, but wins the spirit-world. Instead of penetrating in the I in a way which makes one feel that the sense-world is disappearing, one penetrates into the spirit-world in which one feels the I strengthened.

Furthermore anthroposophy indicates: An experience of destiny exists in which one does not lose the self. In his destiny, one can also realize himself as *active.* In the un-egoistical contemplation of human destiny, anthroposophy provides the experience by which one does not only learn to love one's own existence, but also the world. Instead of staring at the world which carries the I on waves of happiness and despair, one finds the I that designs its own destiny through willing. Instead of ramming against the world by which the I is shattered, he pushes through to his Self and feels united with world events.

Man's destiny is prepared by the world which his senses reveal. If he finds his own activity in the events of destiny, his self does not only arise from his own inner being, but also from the sense-world.

If one can even vaguely feel how the world appears as spiritual in the self and how in the sense-world the self proves to be active, one is already on a sure path to understanding anthroposophy.

For then he will develop awareness that the spirit-world may be described by anthroposophy, which is then grasped by the self. And this awareness will also develop an understanding for the fact that in the sense-world the self can be found in a different way than that of sinking into one's interior. Anthroposophy finds the self by showing how not only sense perceptions are revealed by the sense-world, but also the consequences of previous existence and previous earth-lives.

One can gaze out into the sense world and say: "Here is not only color, sound, warmth; here the soul's experiences work which this soul has lived through during its present earthly existence." And he can look into himself and say: "Here is not only my I; here a spiritual world reveals itself."

By means of such understanding the person touched by the World-Man riddle can find himself together with an initiate who, according to his insights, speaks of the outer sense-world as where not only sense perceptions are made manifest, but also the impressions about what human souls have done in their previous existence and previous earth lives; and who must describe the inner Self-World as revealing spiritual relationships which are as extraordinary and effective as those of the sense-world.

The members who wish to be active should consciously synchronize what the questioning human soul feels as the World-Man riddle with what initiate knowledge has to say when it reveals a bygone world, and when it provides an apperception of a spirit-world through the strengthening of the soul.

By working in this way, the members who wish to be active can make the Anthroposophical Society into a true pre-school of the initiates' school. The Christmas Conference wished to forcefully indicate this; and whoever correctly understands that Conference will continue to carry out this indication until a sufficient understanding can again give the Society new tasks.

The following Guidelines refer to this indication.

62. Sense perception reveals only a superficial part of the being which the sense world hides under the waves of its depths. Through vivid spiritual observation of these depths, the effects of human souls' actions in long bygone times are revealed.

63. The human inner-world reveals to ordinary self-observation only a part of the realm in which it stands. Through strengthened observation it shows that it exists within a living spiritual reality.

64. In man's destiny not only the activities of an external world are manifest, but also those of his Self.

65. In human soul-experiences not merely a Self is manifest, but also a spirit-world. The Self, through spiritualized cognition, is able to recognize that world's solidarity with its own being.

66. The beings of the third hierarchy manifest themselves as the spiritual background to the life which emerges in human thinking. This life is hidden in human thinking activity. If it continued being active as itself, man could not attain to freedom. Human thinking begins where cosmic thinking ends.

67. The beings of the second hierarchy manifest themselves as a psychic element which is beyond humanity. Being of a cosmic-psychic nature, it is hidden from human sensibility. This cosmic-psychic nature acts in the background of human feeling. It transforms the human essence into a feeling organism in order that feeling can live in it.

68. The beings of the first hierarchy manifest themselves in a spiritual creativity which is beyond humanity. As a cosmic-spiritual world of being, it indwells the human will. These cosmic-spiritual beings experience themselves as creative in that man wills. They form the connection between the human being and the external-to-humanity world in order that man may become a free, volitional being.

Spiritual Realms and Human Self-knowledge

The Guidelines which have been sent from the Goetheanum to the members of the Anthroposophical Society during the past weeks link the psychic gaze to the beings of the spiritual realms, to which man is related above just as much as he is to the natural realms below.

True self-knowledge can be the guide to these spiritual realms. And when such self-knowledge is striven for in the right way, one will find understanding for what anthroposophy imparts as knowledge derived from insight into the life of the spiritual world. One must only practice self-knowledge in the right way, and not by merely concentrating on the "inner self".

By means of such real self-knowledge, at first one encounters what is alive in *remembrance*. In thought-pictures he recalls to consciousness the shadows of what he directly experienced in the past. Upon seeing a shadow, one is directed by an inner urge of thinking to the object which cast the shadow. Whoever has a remembrance of something cannot arrive so directly in his mind at the experience which persists in the remembrance. But if he really reflects on his own being, he will have to say: "It is himself, in his soul, who created the experience which cast its shadow and made him what he is." The remembrance-shadows arise in consciousness, and they are *illuminated* in the soul. Dead shadows live in remembrance; living Being resides in the soul in which remembrance continues to act.

One must only be clear about the relationship of remembrance to true soul-life; and in this striving for clarity in self-knowledge one will feel that he is on the path to the spiritual world. Through remembrance one is looking at the spiritual aspect of his own soul. For normal consciousness this visualization does not truly grasp the object. One looks at something, but does not encounter reality.

By means of imaginative cognition, anthroposophy points to this reality. It guides us from shadow to illumination. It does this when speaking of man's *etheric body*. It shows how the physical body acts in the thought-shadow-images; but how the etheric body *lives* in illumination. With his physical body man is in the sense-world, with his etheric body he is in the etheric world. He has an environment in the physical world; he also has one in the etheric world. Anthroposophy refers to this environment as the first hidden world in which man finds himself. It is the realm of the *third hierarchy*.

We approach *language* in the same way we approached remembrance. It arises from within man, as does remembrance. Through it man connects to a being as he does in respect to his own experiences in remembrance. A shadow nature is also present in words. It is stronger than the shadow nature of remembrance. When a person casts the shadow from his experiences in remembrance, his hidden self in active in the whole process. He is present as illumination casts the shadow.

There is also a shadow-casting in language. Words are shadows. What illumines here? Something stronger illumines, for words are stronger shadows than remembrances. What remembrances can create in the human self during the course of an earth life cannot create words. He must learn them in relationship with others. A deeper being in him than the one casting remembrance shadows must participate. Here anthroposophy speaks from inspired cognition of the astral body, as it does of the etheric body in respect to remembrance. The astral body is thus added to the physical and etheric bodies as the human being's third component.

This third member also has a cosmic environment. It is that of the *second hierarchy*. A shadow-image of this second hierarchy is given in human speech. Man lives with his astral body within the realm of this hierarchy.

We can go further. In speaking man participates with part of his being; he puts his inner self in motion. What surrounds his inner self remains in repose in speech itself. The motion involved in speaking wrests itself from the human being in repose. But the whole man goes into motion when he activates his limbs. In this movement he is no less expressive than in remembrance and speech. Remembrance expresses experiences; the essence of speech is that it expresses something. Thus man in movement with his whole being expresses a "something".

Anthroposophy describes what is thus expressed as an additional component of the human being. Through intuitive cognition it speaks

24

of the "true self" or the "I". It also finds its cosmic environment: that of the *first hierarchy*.

By moving toward his remembrance-thoughts, man is met by a primary super-sensible component, his own etheric being. By grasping himself as a speaker, his astral being comes to meet him. This is no longer grasped only by what acts inwardly, like remembrance. Inspiration sees it as that which, in speaking, forms a physical act that originates in the spirit. Speech is a physical process. Fundamentally it is a function from the realm of the second hierarchy.

In the whole man in motion a more intensive physical action is present than in speaking. It is not "something" which is formed; it is the whole person. Here the first hierarchy is active in the formation of the active physical human being.

In this way true self-knowledge can be practiced. One does not grasp his own self alone in this way however. Gradually he grasps his component members: the physical body, the etheric body, the astral body, the self. And in grasping these elements, he gradually approaches the higher worlds in which his being unfolds — just as the three kingdoms of nature: the animal, the vegetable, the mineral belong as three spiritual realms to the cosmos as a whole.

69. The third hierarchy manifests itself as pure spirit-soul. It acts in what man experiences psychically, that is, in his soul. Processes could take place neither in the etheric nor in the astral regions if only this hierarchy was active. Only the spiritual-psychic would exist.

70. The second hierarchy manifests itself as the spiritual-psychic which acts in the etheric. Everything etheric is a manifestation of the second hierarchy. It manifests itself only indirectly in the physical however. Its strength extends only to etheric processes. Only the psychic and the etheric would exist if the third and second hierarchies alone were active.

71. The first hierarchy, the strongest, manifests itself as spiritually active in the physical. It transforms the physical world into Cosmos. The third and the second hierarchies serve as helpers.

72. As soon as one approaches the higher components of the human being: the etheric and astral bodies and the I-organization, he feels impelled to seek the relation of man to the beings of the spiritual realms. Only the physical-body organization can be illumined by the three physical kingdoms of nature.

73. Cosmic intelligence is integrated in the human being in the etheric body. In order for this to happen, the activity of cosmic beings is required who, cooperating, shape the etheric body, just as the physical forces shape the physical.

74. The spiritual world impresses moral impulses in the human being. Their effectiveness depends upon the activity of beings who not only think the spiritual, but can also essentially shape it.

75. In the I-organization, man experiences himself in the physical body as spirit. In order for this to happen, the activity of beings is necessary who themselves live in the physical world as spiritual beings.

How the Guidelines are to be used:

The Guidelines issued from the Goetheanum are meant to motivate the members who wish to be active to give the content of anthroposophical activity an integrative form. They will find that by considering these guidelines every week, they provide guidance for deepening their understanding of the material already given in the lecture cycles, and enable them to present them at branch meetings in a more orderly fashion.

It would certainly be preferable if every week the lectures given in Dornach could be immediately communicated to all the branches. But one can imagine the complicated technical arrangements necessary to do this. The Executive Board is doing everything possible in this direction. But we must take the available possibilities into account. The intentions presented at the Christmas Conference will be realized. But we need time.

Presently the branches which have members who visit the Goetheanum and hear the lectures and can communicate their content to the branches have an advantage. And the branches should realize that sending those members to the Goetheanum is beneficial. But one should not undervalue the work which has already been accomplished in the Anthroposophical Society and which is available in the printed courses and lectures. Whoever examines these lecture cycles and remembers what content is in one or the other according to the titles, and then goes to the Guidelines, will find that what is contained in the various lecture cycles is elaborated further in the Guidelines. By reading them together, the viewpoints which are separated in the individual cycles can be illustrated and explained with the support of the Guidelines.

It is wasteful if we leave the printed cycles unused and are only interested in "the newest" from the Goetheanum. It is also easy to understand that the ability to print the cycles will gradually end if they are not used extensively.

Another point comes into question here. In the dissemination of anthroposophical content, conscientiousness and a sense of responsibility are of prime importance. One must transmit what is said about the spiritual world in images of spiritual facts and beings in a way which does not give rise to misunderstandings. If someone hears a lecture at the Goetheanum, he receives a direct impression of it. When he then imparts it to others this impression lingers, and he is able to formulate the things so that they are correctly understood. If a second or even a third person becomes the intermediary however, the probability increases that inaccuracies creep in. This should be kept in mind.

And a third viewpoint is the most important. It is not a question of anthroposophical content being merely listened to or read, but that it be assimilated by the living soul. What is essential lies in the continuous thinking about and feeling what has been has been received. This is meant to be stimulated by the Guidelines in respect to the already available printed lecture cycles. If this viewpoint is disregarded, it will become ever more difficult for the Being of anthroposophy to be revealed through the Anthroposophical Society.

One says with apparent justification: "What good is it to me to hear so much about spiritual worlds if I can't see into those worlds myself?" This does not take into consideration the fact that the ability to see is furthered when anthroposophical content is treated as indicated here. The lectures at the Goetheanum are given in such a way that their content can livingly and freely be retained in the listeners' hearts. It is no dead material for the mere passing on of information. It is of a substance which by various viewpoints stimulates the ability to see into spiritual worlds. One should not believe: I listen to the lectures; I acquire knowledge of the spiritual world through meditation. One will never really progress in that way. Both must work together into the soul. And continuous thinking and feeling anthroposophical content is also practice for the soul. One lives *seeing* into the spiritual world if one proceeds with this content in the way indicated here.

In the Anthroposophical Society it is not sufficiently understood that anthroposophy is not some bleak theory, but is meant to be true life. True life, that is its essence; and when it is *made* into a bleak theory it is often not a *better* theory than others, but a *worse* one. But it is transformed into a theory when it is made into one, when it is killed. It is not sufficiently understood that anthroposophy is not merely a different worldview than others, but that *it must also be assimilated differently*. One recognizes and experiences its essence by this different way of assimilating it.

The Goetheanum should be recognized as the *necessary* center of anthroposophical activity; but one must not forget that in the branches the anthroposophical material which has been elaborated here should also be utilized. What has been elaborated at the Goetheanum can be acquired *gradually* by the whole Anthroposophical Society in a completely vital sense, if as many branch members as possible come to the Goetheanum and participate in *its* living activity. It must all, however, be done introspectively; merely "communicating" the contents every week is not acceptable. The Executive Committee at the Goetheanum will need time and understanding from the members. Then we *will* be able to carry out the intentions of the Christmas Conference.

76. If one wishes to evoke a mental image of the first hierarchy (Seraphim, Cherubim and Thrones), one must try to form images in which the spiritual (only supersensibly visible) is actively manifested in the form in which they appear in the sense-world.

The spiritual as sense-perceptible imagery must be the content of our thoughts about the first hierarchy.

77. If one wishes to evoke a mental image of the second hierarchy (Kyriotetes, Dynameis, Exusiai), one must try to form images in which the spiritual is manifested not in sense-perceptible forms, but in a purely spiritual way. The spiritual in non-sense perceptible, purely spiritual imagery must be the content of thoughts about the second hierarchy.

78. If one wishes to evoke a mental image of the third hierarchy (Archai, Archangeloi, Angeloi), one must try to form images in which the spiritual is manifested neither in sense-perceptible forms nor in a purely spiritual way, but rather as thinking, feeling and willing act in the human soul. The spiritual as psychic [soul] imagery must be the content of thoughts about a third hierarchy.

At the Dawn of the Michael Age

Up until the ninth century after the mystery of Golgotha, man's relation to his thinking was different than afterward. He did not feel that the thoughts which lived in his mind* were of his own making. He considered them to be inspirations from a spiritual world. Even when he had thoughts deriving from his sense perceptions, these thoughts were, for him, revelations from the divine which spoke to him through the senses.

Whoever has spiritual vision will understand this feeling. For when a spiritual reality informs his soul, he never feels that he has formed the thoughts needed to grasp the spiritual perception, but he *envisions* the thoughts which are contained in the perception as objectively as the perception itself.

With the ninth century (of course such dates are to be understood as being approximate, the transitions occurring gradually) the spark of personal-individual intelligence ignited. Man had the feeling: *I form* my thoughts. And this forming of thoughts became the most important element in his soul life, so that the thinkers saw the essence of the human soul in intelligent behavior. Previously they had an imaginative conception of the soul. They didn't see its essence in the forming of thoughts, but in its participation in the spiritual content of the world. They considered that super-sensible spiritual beings were thinking in them. Soul for them was what lives in man from the super-sensible spiritual world.

From the moment one penetrates with perception into the spiritual world, he encounters authentic spiritual beings. According to ancient teachings, the power from which the thoughts about things flow was known by the name *Michael.* The name can be retained. For one can say: once human beings received thoughts from Michael. Michael governed cosmic intelligence. From the ninth century on, people no longer felt that Michael inspired their thoughts. They had escaped his domination; they fell from the spiritual world into individual human minds.

From then on thoughts would evolve within humanity. At first people were uncertain as to what they now possessed. This

31

uncertainty inhabited the scholastic teachings. The scholastics were divided between realists and nominalists. The realists — led by Thomas of Aquinas and those close to him — felt the old connection between thought and thing. They therefore saw reality in the thoughts that lived in things. They viewed human thoughts as reality which flowed from things into the mind. The nominalists strongly felt that the mind forms the thoughts. They considered thoughts to be only subjective — which live in the mind and which have nothing to do with things. They opined that thoughts were only names invented by men for the things. (They didn't speak about "thoughts", but "universals"; but that is irrelevant in principle, for thoughts always have something universal compared to the individual thing.)

One can say: The realists wanted to be true to Michael even though thoughts had fallen from his realm into that of man. As thinkers they wanted to serve Michael as the Prince of Cosmic Intelligence. — The nominalists in their unconscious minds fulfilled the separation from Michael. They considered man rather than Michael to be the owner of thoughts.

Nominalism gained in diffusion and influence. This situation prevailed up until the last third of the nineteenth century. At that time, those people who understood the events in the universe felt that Michael had accompanied the stream of intellectual life. He sought a new metamorphoses of his cosmic task. Previously he let the thoughts from the spiritual world flow into human souls; from the last third of the nineteenth century on he wants to live *in* human souls in which thoughts are formed. Previously the people related to Michael saw him unfold his activities in the spirit-world; now they realized that they should allow Michael to reside in their hearts; they dedicated their thought-filled spiritual life to him; now in free, individual thinking life, they let themselves be instructed by Michael as to the soul's right path.

Human beings who in their previous earth-lives were inspired by Michael in their thinking, who were therefore Michael's servants, felt themselves attracted to such voluntary Michael associations at the end of the nineteenth century when they again lived on earth. From then on they considered their old instigator of thoughts to be the guide to higher thoughts.

He who is able to value such things knows what a transformation took place during the last third of the nineteenth century in respect to human thinking. Previously man could only feel how thoughts formed from within his being; from the above-mentioned time he was able to lift himself above his being; he could turn meaning towards the spiritual; Michael meets him there, and shows himself to be related to all thinking activity. He frees thoughts from the region of the head; he clears the way to the heart for them. He liberates enthusiasm from feeling, so that man can mindfully dedicate himself to all which he can experience in the *light of thoughts.* The Michael age has dawned. Hearts begin to have thoughts; enthusiasm no longer streams from mere mystical obscurity, but from thinking endowed with clarity of mind. To understand this means to receive Michael in one's sensibility. Thoughts which today strive towards grasping the spiritual must come from hearts which beat for Michael as the fiery Prince of Thought of the Universe.

* In the original German the word "Seele" (soul) is used. However, in much of the context of these paragraphs the word "mind" — which does not exist in German — would normally be used in English. I have therefore (rather shakily) substituted mind for soul wherever I deemed appropriate. Wherever "mind" appears above, the reader should perhaps realize that the original reads "soul". (Trans.)

79. One can spiritually approach the third hierarchy (Archai, Archangeloi, Angeloi) when one becomes so acquainted with thinking, feeling and willing that he sees in them the spirit being active in the soul. At first thinking places only *images* in the world, not something real. Feeling moves in this imagery, speaking for reality in man, but cannot fully manifest it. Willing unfolds a reality, which requires the body, but which does not act consciously in its formation. What is essential in thinking in order to make the body the basis of this thinking, what is essential in feeling to make the body a participant in a reality, what is essential in willing in order to consciously participate in the body's formation — is alive in the third hierarchy.

80. One can spiritually approach the second hierarchy (Exusiai, Dynameis, Kyriotetes) when one envisions the facts of nature as manifestations of the living spirit in them. The second hierarchy, then, has nature as its residence, in order to work in it on souls.

81. One can spiritually approach the first hierarchy (Seraphim, Cherubim, Thrones) when one envisions the facts of nature and human life as the deeds (creations) of the spirit acting in them. The first hierarchy, then, has the natural and human realms as the scene of its unfolding activity.

82. Man gazes up at the star-worlds; what he sees is the external manifestation of the spiritual beings and their deeds, of which we spoke in the previous considerations as the beings of the spiritual realms (hierarchies).

83. The earth is the stage for the three realms of nature and the human realm, insofar as they manifest the deeds of spiritual beings to the external senses.

84. The forces which work into the earthly realms of nature and humanity by spiritual beings reveal themselves to the human spirit through true, spiritual knowledge of the star-worlds.

The State of the Human Soul before the Michael Age

Today we will add a consideration of the ideas which relate to "At the Dawn of the Michael Age". The Michael age has arisen in the evolution of humanity after the predominance of intellectual thinking on the one hand and that of human perception directed towards the external sense-world — the physical world — on the other.

Thinking is *not* essentially a development towards materialism. The world of ideas, which in older times had come to man as inspiration, became the property of the human mind in the period which preceded the Michael age. It no longer receives ideas "from above", from the spiritual content of the cosmos, but conceives them from man's own spirituality. For the first time man has become sufficiently mature to contemplate his own spiritual being. Previously he had not penetrated so deeply into his own nature. He saw himself as a drop separated from the spiritual cosmic sea in order to live on earth and eventually to be reunited with that cosmos.

This process of thought formation now constitutes an enhancement of human self-knowledge. Viewed supersensibly it looks like this: The spiritual powers, which we may designate as "Michael", govern the ideas in the spiritual cosmos. Man experienced these ideas in that his soul participated in the Michael-world. This experiencing has now become his own. A temporary separation from the Michael-world has therewith occurred. Previously by means of inspired thoughts man received at the same time the spiritual cosmic content. When this inspiration ended, he became dependent upon the senses in order to have content for his thoughts. Therefore the content of the spirituality he had obtained had to be suffused with materialism. He fell into the materialistic viewpoint at a time when his own spiritual being advanced to a higher stage than the previous one.

This is easily misunderstood; one can consider only the "fall" into materialism and rue it. But whereas *perception* during this age had to be limited to the external physical world, within the soul a *purified, self-subsisting spirituality* developed as *experience*. In the Michael Age the experience no longer needs to be unconscious, but can become conscious of its nature. This means the entrance into the human soul of the Michael essence. During a certain time man filled his spirit with the material content of nature; he should now fill it again with the cosmic content of his original spirituality.

Thinking lost itself for a while in the materiality of the cosmos; it must find itself again in the cosmic spirit. Warmth — being-filled spirit-reality — can enter into the cold, abstract thought-world. This characterizes the Dawn of the Michael Age.

It was only by separation from the universal thinking essence could consciousness of freedom develop in the depths of the human soul. What came from the heights had to be rediscovered in the depths. Therefore, the development of this consciousness of freedom was originally oriented only to knowledge of external nature. While man was unconsciously learning to mold purity of ideas within his spirit, his senses were directed outward towards the material world, which in no way affected the tender seed germinating in his soul.

But in perceiving the exterior material world, experiencing the spirit and therewith spiritual *seeing* can be introduced in a new way. What has been learned about nature under the sign of materialism can be spiritually grasped by the inner life of the soul. Michael, who spoke "from above", can be heard "from within", where he will now take up residence. Speaking imaginatively this can be expressed thus: the sun-quality, which man for a long time only received from the cosmos, will shine from within the soul. He will learn to speak of an "inner sun". In life between birth and death he will of course be no less an earth-being; but he will recognize his developing being as *guided by the sun.* He will feel as truth that an essence shines a light on him from within, but one which is not kindled there. At the Dawn of the Michael Age it may still seem as though all this is far beyond humanity; However, it is near "in the spirit"; it must only be "seen".

Immeasurably much depends upon this fact: that man's ideas are not merely "thought", but are also "seen".

85. During the present cosmic era, man experiences himself in waking consciousness. This experiencing conceals from him the presence of the third hierarchy within his wakefulness.

86. In dream consciousness, man experiences his own being united with the spiritual essence of the universe in a chaotic way. If Imagination is placed as the other pole to this dream consciousness, man would realize that the second hierarchy is present in his experience.

87. In the consciousness of dreamless sleep man experiences his own being united with the spiritual essence of the universe, but without his conscious knowledge. If Inspiration is placed as the other pole to this consciousness of dreamless sleep, he would realize that the first hierarchy is present in his experience.

Aphorisms

from a lecture for members given on
August 24, 1924 in London:

At the present stage of its development human consciousness develops three forms, the waking, the dreaming and the dreamless sleeping consciousness.

Waking consciousness experiences the sensory outer world, forms ideas about it and can create from these ideas those which depict a purely spiritual world. Dreaming consciousness develops images which transform the outer world — for example, the sun shining on a bed can become a great fire with many details. Or it presents one's inner world in symbolic pictures to the soul — for example a strongly beating heart in the image of an overheated oven. Memories also appear transformed in dream consciousness. The content of such images, which do not derive from the sensory but from the spiritual world, nevertheless do not provide the possibility to knowingly penetrate into the spiritual world because their dimness does not allow them to be completely raised to waking consciousness, and because what does get through cannot be readily grasped.

It is possible, however, directly upon waking from the dream world, to grasp enough to recognize that it is the imperfect impression of a spiritual experience that pervades sleep, but which for the most part evades waking consciousness. In order to see this clearly it is only necessary to shape the moment of waking so that it doesn't invoke the outer world to the mind in one beat, but so that the mind, without looking outward, concentrates on the inner experience.

Dreamless sleep consciousness lets the soul pass through experiences which in memory appear as only undifferentiated events in time. One will speak of these experiences as being non-existent as long as one does not access them through spiritual-scientific investigation. If this is done however, one develops imaginative and inspired consciousness, as described in anthroposophical literature, for the pictures and the inspirations of experiences from previous earth lives rise to the surface. And then one can comprehend the content of dream consciousness. It is a content which is incomprehensible to waking consciousness, for it applies to the world in which man sojourns as a disembodied soul between two earth lives.

If one learns what is hidden in dream and sleeping consciousness during the contemporary stage of world evolution, then the way will be opened to knowledge of the evolutionary forms of human consciousness during previous stages. On cannot, however, achieve this by means of external research. For the evidence thus obtained only indicates the aftereffects of human consciousness's prehistoric experiences. Anthroposophical literature provides information on how to achieve a vision of such experiences through spiritual research.

This research finds that in ancient Egyptian times dream-consciousness was much closer to waking consciousness than is the case today. Memories of the dream experiences streamed into waking consciousness, which presented not merely the sensory impressions in clearly contoured thoughts, but also, united with these thoughts, the spirit which acts in the sensory world. In this way man and his consciousness existed instinctively in the [spiritual] world which he had abandoned during his earthly incarnation and which he would again enter upon passing through the portal of death.

Objective study of the writing in monuments and elsewhere clearly indicates the existence of such a consciousness, which belonged to a time when external records did not exist.

Sleep-consciousness in ancient Egyptian times contained dreams of the spiritual world in a way similar to the present-day dreams which contain elements derived from the physical world.

One finds, however, still another consciousness in other peoples. Sleep streamed its experiences into wakefulness in such a way that a vision of previous earth lives was instinctively present. Ancient people's traditional knowledge of repeated earth lives originated from this form of consciousness.

One finds again in developed imaginative cognition what in ancient times was a dimly instinctive dream-consciousness. But now it is a fully waking consciousness.

And one is also aware through inspired cognition of the ancient instinctive insight which still saw something of repeated earth lives. Present day historical scholarship does not take note of this development of human forms of consciousness. It prefers to believe that contemporary consciousness forms were present as long as earthly humanity existed.

And evidence of such different consciousness forms as is contained in myths and fairy tales they take to be the result of an outflow of ancient man's poetic fantasy.

88. In the waking consciousness of present times man experiences himself as standing within the physical world. This experience hides from him the fact that within his own being the effects of a life between death and birth are active.

89. In dreaming consciousness man experiences his own being unharmoniously united with the spiritual being of the universe in a chaotic way. Waking consciousness cannot grasp the essential content of this dreaming consciousness. Imaginative and inspired consciousness reveals that the spiritual world, through which man lives between death and birth, participates in the formation of his inner being.

90. In the consciousness of dreamless sleep man experiences his own being — without conscious knowledge — as infused with the results of previous earth-lives. Inspired and intuitive consciousness progress towards the revelation of these results and see the activity of previous lives in the pattern of destiny (karma) in the present life.

91. The will enters normal consciousness only through thoughts in the present era. This normal consciousness can only relate to what is sensibly perceptible however. It grasps only what is perceptible through the senses about its own nature. In this consciousness man knows about his impulses of will only by the

thinking observation of himself, as he knows of the outer world only by observing it.

92. Karma, which is active in the will, is an inherent attribute in it from previous earth lives. It cannot, therefore, be grasped by ideas derived from sensory existence, which are only oriented towards contemporary earth life.

93. Because these ideas cannot grasp karma, they relegate what is unintelligible about human will impulses to the mystical obscurity of the bodily constitution, whereas in reality it is the effect of past earth lives.

94. Man stands in the physical world with ordinary conceptualization which is imparted through the senses. In order to incorporate this physical world into his consciousness, karma must be silent. In a manner of speaking man, as a thinker, *forgets* his karma.

95. Karma acts in manifestations of will. But its activity remains unconscious. By advancing to Imagination that which is unconsciously active in the will, karma is grasped. One feels his destiny internally.

96. Once Inspiration and Intuition join Imagination, in addition to the impulses of the present, the effect of former earth lives is also perceptible in the activity of the will. Past life actively manifests itself in the present one.

97. A cruder description might say: *thinking, feeling* and *willing* live in the human soul. A subtler one must say: thinking always contains an undercoating of feeling and willing; feeling of thinking and willing; willing of thinking and feeling. It is just that the thinking aspect predominates in thought, as do feeling and willing in their respective domains.

98. The feeling and willing of thought contain the karmic results of past earth lives. The thinking and willing of feeling determine character in a karmic way. The thinking and feeling of willing wrench the current earth-life from its karmic connections.

99. In the feeling and willing of thinking man lives out the karma of the past; in the thinking and feeling of the will he prepares the karma of the future.

100. Thoughts have their actual seat in the human etheric body. But there they are living essential forces. They impress themselves on the physical body. And as such "impressed thoughts" they have the shadowy quality through which normal consciousness knows them.

101. What lives in thoughts as feeling comes from the astral body, what lives as willing comes from the "I". In sleep the human etheric body radiates with one's thoughts; only the person does not participate, for he has extracted — from the etheric and physical bodies — the feeling of thoughts with the astral body, and the willing of same with the "I".

102. At the moment during sleep in which the astral body and the I sever their relation to the etheric body's thoughts, they enter into relation with "karma" — to envisioning the events throughout repeated earth-lives. This envisioning is not open to normal consciousness — [unless] a super-sensible consciousness enters it.

The Pre-Michaelic and the Michaelic Path

One will not be able to see in the right light how the Michael impulse entered into human evolution if one thinks about the relationship between the new ideas and nature in the way which is usual today.

One thinks: out there is nature with its processes and beings; within there are the ideas which describe concepts about nature or also the so-called laws of nature. For the thinkers it's all about how *these* ideas are formed which have a correct relation to nature or contain the true laws of nature.

Little importance is given to how these ideas relate to the person who has them. Nevertheless, one will only understand what is important when the question is asked: What does man experience in the new natural-scientific ideas?

The answer may be found in the following way.

Today man considers that his ideas have arisen through the activity of his soul [mind]. He feels that he is the architect of his ideas, whereas only the perceptions come to him from without.

He did not always feel this way. In older times he did not feel that the content of ideas was self-made, but rather something received as inspiration from the super-sensible world.

This feeling came about by stages. And the stages depended upon which part of his being experienced what he calls his ideas today. In today's age of Consciousness Soul development, what is stated in the previous guidelines is unreservedly valid: "Thoughts have their actual seat in the human etheric body. But there they are living, essential forces. They impress themselves on the physical body. And as such 'impressed thoughts' they have the shadowy quality through which normal consciousness knows them."

One could go back to the time when thoughts were directly experienced in the "I". Then they were not shadowy as today; they weren't merely *living*; they were *ensouled* and thoroughly *spiritualized.* But that means: Man did *not think* thoughts; rather he experienced the perception of actual spiritual beings.

***

Everywhere in antiquity one would find a consciousness which looked up to such a world of spiritual beings. What has been historically retained of this is called myth-building consciousness today, and no particular value is attributed to it for understanding the real world. Yet man stands with this consciousness in *his* world, in the world of his origin, while he extracts himself from this, *his* world with today's consciousness.

Man is spirit. And *his* world is that of the spirits.

A next stage is where thinking was no longer experienced by the "I", but by the astral body. Here direct spirituality was lost to the mind's view. Thought appeared as an ensouled living thing.

During the first stage, that of seeing actual spiritual beings, man did not strongly feel the need to relate what was spiritually seen to the sense-perceptible world. Although the sensory phenomena manifested themselves to him as super-sensible acts, there was no necessity to create a special science for what the "spiritual view" directly perceived. Furthermore, the spiritual beings' world was of such magnitude that attention was directed there above all.

It was different during the second consciousness stage, when the actual spiritual beings hid themselves from view; their reflection, as ensouled life, appeared. One began to associate the "life of nature" with this "life of soul". One sought the active spiritual essence and its deeds in nature and natural phenomena. What later appeared as alchemy is to be seen as an historical echo of this consciousness stage.

Just as man "thought" spirit-beings during the first consciousness stage, living completely in *his* being, in this second stage he was still close to himself and his spiritual origins.

It was quite impossible at both stages for him to really arrive at his own inner impulse to action.

A spirituality which is of his own nature acted in him. What *he* seemed to do was the manifestation of processes which occurred through spiritual beings. What the person did was the sensory-physical emergence of a real divine-spiritual occurrence behind it.

A third epoch of consciousness evolution brought thoughts to consciousness, but as living ones in the etheric body.

When the Greek civilization was great it lived in this consciousness. When the Greek thought, he did not form a thought through which he, as if of his own shaping, looked at the world. Rather he felt a life evoked which also pulsated externally in things and processes.

Therewith the desire for freedom of his own actions arose for the first time; not yet true freedom, but the desire for it.

Man, who felt the actions of nature within him, was able to develop the desire to emancipate his own activity from an activity he perceived to be a foreign to him. Nevertheless, he still felt the last vestiges of the spirit-world — which is of the same nature as man — in exterior activity.

It was only once the thoughts impregnated themselves in the physical body and consciousness extended to this limit, was the possibility of freedom realized. This was the situation during the fifteenth century.

The evolution of the world does not depend on the what importance the current ideas about nature may have; for these ideas have not taken the form they have in order to deliver a certain image of nature, but to bring humanity to a certain stage of development.

When thoughts captured the physical body — spirit, soul and life were excised from their content; and the abstract shadows which clung to the physical body alone remained. Such thoughts can *only* make physical-material elements the objects of their cognition. For they themselves are only *real* in the physical-material body of man.

Materialism did not arise because only material beings and processes are perceivable in nature, but because man had to pass through a stage in his evolution which led him to a consciousness in which he was initially only capable of seeing material manifestations. This necessary one-sided organization of human evolution resulted in the modern conception of nature.

Michael's mission is to bring the forces to human etheric bodies through which the shadow-thoughts can regain *life*; then the souls and spirits of the super-sensible world will be drawn towards the invigorated thoughts; liberated man will be able to live with them, as formerly when he was only the physical reflection of *their* activity, lived with them.

103. In the evolution of humanity, consciousness descends the ladder of thought development. During the first consciousness stage man experienced thoughts in the "I" as spiritual, ensouled, enlivened essence. During the second stage, man experienced thoughts in the astral body; they manifested there only a greater degree of the ensouled and enlivened spiritual essence. During the third stage, man experienced thought in the etheric body; they manifested only an inner activity, like an echo of soul. During the fourth, contemporary stage, man experiences thoughts in the physical body; they manifest dead shadows of the spiritual.

104. To the degree that the spirit-soul enlivened thinking retreats, man's self-will comes to life — and freedom becomes possible.

105. Michael's task is to lead man back on the pathway of will from whence he came, for he descended on the pathway of thinking from super-sensory experience to sensory experience with his earthly consciousness.

Michael's Task in the Sphere of Ahriman

When man looks back upon his evolution and the special attributes which brought him to the spiritual vision which his spiritual life has taken on during the past five hundred years, he *must*, even with normal consciousness, at least recognize that since these five hundred years he has stood at an important turning-point in the earthly evolution of humanity.

In the previous consideration, I pointed to this important turning-point from *one* point of view — the observation of evolution in antiquity. One sees how the soul-force in man developed to the point where it is now active as the force of intelligence.

Dead, abstract thoughts now appear in the field of human consciousness. These thoughts are bound to man's physical body, and he must recognize that they are of his own making.

In antiquity man saw divine-spiritual beings when directing his vision to where his own thoughts originated. He found his whole being, down to the physical body, bound to these beings; he had to recognize himself as their creation — but as such creation not only recognize his *being*, but also his *deeds*. Man had no will of his own. What he did was the manifestation of divine will.

In stages, as has been described, he has come to have his own will, beginning approximately five hundred years ago. But the last stage is far more different from all the others than they are amongst themselves.

In that thoughts pass over to the physical body, they lose life. They become dead; spiritually dead structures. Previously, as they belonged to man, they were simultaneously organs of the divine-spiritual beings to whom man belonged. They *willed* in man. And therefore through them man felt himself united with the spiritual world.

With dead thoughts he feels himself detached from the spiritual world. He feels himself completely displaced to the physical world.

He is thus displaced to the sphere of ahrimanic spirituality. This has no strong power in the areas in which the beings of the higher hierarchies keep man in *their* sphere, in which they either act in man themselves, as in antiquity or, as later, through their ensouled or living reflection. As long as super-sensible beings acted in human affairs, that is until the fifteenth century, the ahrimanic powers had only a weakly suggestive power *within human evolution.* Direct intervention only became possible in the period that began approximately five-hundred years ago.

The Persian worldview did not contradict this when describing Ahriman's work. For that worldview did not imply Ahriman working within human soul-evolution, but in one directly bordering on the human soul-world. Ahriman's machinations may have run over from a neighboring spirit-world into the human soul-world, but did not directly intervene.

Thus man stands at the end of an evolutionary stream in which his being, derived from such a divine-spirituality, finally succumbs, as such, to his abstract intelligence.

Man has not remained in the divine-spiritual spheres which constitute his origin. What began five-hundred years ago for human consciousness had already taken place to a larger extent for his whole being when the Mystery of Golgotha took place on earth. Imperceptibly for the consciousness of most people, human evolution had gradually slipped out of a world in which Ahriman had little power into one in which he had much. This slipping into a different world-stratum reached its completion in the fifteenth century.

Ahriman's influence on humanity during that world-stratum was possible and could have had devastating consequences, because in that stratum man's relation to divine activity had died out. But man could not develop free will in any other way than by making his way into a sphere in which the divine-spiritual beings that had been united with him from the very beginning were not living.

Seen cosmically, the Sun-Mystery is in the essence of human evolution. Up until the important turning-point of his evolution, man was able to perceive that divine-spiritual beings were conjoined with his origin. *They* have however detached themselves from the sun and left only what is dead behind. So that man in his corporality can now only receive dead thoughts through the sun.

But those beings have sent Christ from the sun to the earth. He has united his being with the mortality of the divine-spiritual existence in Ahriman's realm for the healing of humanity. Thus humanity has two possibilities that guarantee his freedom: to consciously turn to Christ with the spiritual disposition he subconsciously held during the descent from the vision of super-sensory spirituality up until the use of the intellect; or to complete the detachment from this spirituality and therewith become addicted to the orientation of Ahrimanic powers.

Humanity has been in this situation since the beginning of the fifteenth century. This has been in preparation — with evolution everything happens gradually — since the Mystery of Golgotha which, as the earth's greatest event, is intended to rescue man from the corruption he is necessarily exposed to, because he is meant to be a free being.

One can therefore say that what humanity has done in this situation was in semiconsciousness. And in this way it led to what is good in the abstract ideas about nature and to many equally good principles about life in general. But the time is over when man may still unconsciously evolve in the dangerous Ahrimanic sphere.

The investigator of the spiritual world *must* draw humanity's attention to the spiritual fact that Michael has taken over the spiritual leadership of human affairs. Michael does what he must do in a way which does not influence people; but *they* can follow *him* in freedom with the Christ-force, in order to find their way out of Ahriman's sphere in which in was necessary for them to enter.

Whoever honestly feels one with Anthroposophy from the bottom of his soul will rightly understand this Michael phenomenon. And Anthroposophy would like to be the messenger of this Michael-Mission.

106. Michael goes again upward along the paths which humanity trod downward during the stages of spiritual evolution to the activation of intelligence. But Michaelic will lead wills upward along the pathways which wisdom trod downward until its last stage: intelligence.

107. In order than humanity can develop in freedom, from now on in world evolution Michael *merely points out* the path, which differentiates *this* Michael leadership from all earlier archangel leaderships, even from all earlier Michael leaderships. The earlier leaderships *were active* in man — which meant that man's own actions could not be free.

108. To *recognize* this is man's present task, so that he can find his spiritual path with his whole soul during the Michael era.

Michael's Experiences during the Fulfillment of his Cosmic Mission

One can follow the advance of humanity from the consciousness stage when man felt himself to be a member of the divine-spiritual order up until the contemporary stage, where he feels himself to be an individual detached from the divine-spiritual and capable of his own thinking. This was elucidated in the last article.

However, through super-sensible vision one can also project a picture of how Michael and his associates experience this stream of evolution; that is, describe the same facts from Michael's point of view. We will try to do this now.

At first there is an oldest antiquity in which one can only speak of what happened among divine-spiritual beings. It has to do with the deeds of gods alone. Gods accomplish what the impulses of their natures provide; they are correspondingly satisfied with this activity. And only what *they* experience is taken into consideration. Something like humanity is only noticeable in one area of this godly activity. It is an element of godly activity.

The spiritual being who directed his attention to humanity from the beginning, however, is Michel. He arranges divine activity is such a way that humanity can exist in a cosmic corner, so to speak. And the manner in which he acts there is related to the activity that later is manifested in humanity as intellect; except that it is activated as a force which streams through the cosmos in an ordering of ideas, giving rise to reality. Michael works in this force. His office is to administer cosmic intellectuality. He wishes further advancement in this area. And this can only happen if what streams through the cosmos as intelligence is concentrated later in the human individuality. What occurs thereby is the following: a time comes in world evolution in which the cosmos no longer lives by its present intelligence, but by that of its past. And the intelligence of the present is amidst the stream of human evolution.

Michael would like to ensure that what develops within humanity as intelligence continues to be connected to the divine-spiritual beings. To this, however, there is resistance. What the gods accomplish as evolution from the separation of intellectuality from their own cosmic action up until integration in human nature is an open fact in the world. If beings exist who possess a capacity for perceiving these facts, they can make use of them. And such beings do exist. They are the Ahrimanic beings. They are very much disposed to soak up everything separated as intelligence from the gods. They are disposed to unite the sum of all intellectuality to their own being. Thereby they become the greatest, the most comprehensive and penetrating intelligences in the cosmos.

Michael foresees how man, in that he uses his own intelligence ever more, must encounter the Ahrimanic beings and how he can thus succumb to them. Therefore Michael places the Ahrimanic powers under his feet, he continuously forces them into a deeper region than the one in which man is evolving. Michael, the dragon under his feet, forcing him into the abyss: that is the mighty image of this super-sensible fact that lives in human consciousness.

Evolution advances. Intellectuality, which at first was completely in the divine-spiritual domain, is so detached from it that it becomes the ensoulment of the cosmos. What previously radiated only from the gods now blazes forth from the stars as divine revelation. Previously the world was guided through *divine being* itself, now it is guided through objective *divine revelation,* behind which divine being continues on the path of *its* own evolution.

Michael is again the administrator of cosmic intelligence, insofar as it streams through cosmic revelation in ideational form.

The third phase of evolution is a further separation of cosmic intelligence from its origins. In the star-worlds the present complex of ideas no longer rules as divine revelation; the stars move and arrange themselves according to the arrangement implanted in them in the past. Michael sees how what he administered in the cosmos, cosmic intellectuality, increasingly continues along the path to earthly humanity.

Michael also sees, however, that the danger of humanity succumbing to the Ahrimanic powers is ever greater. He knows: he will always have Ahriman under his feet *for himself;* but what about man?

Michael sees the greatest earthly event happening. From the domain which Michael himself served, the Christ-Being descends to the earthly sphere in order to be here when intelligence is completely present in the human individuality. This is when man will most strongly feel the pressure to become addicted to the power which has completely and absolutely become the bearer of intellectuality. But Christ will be there; through his great sacrifice he will live in the same sphere in which Ahriman lives. Humanity will be able to choose between Christ and Ahriman. The world will be able to find the Christ-path in human evolution.

That is Michael's cosmic experience of what he has to administer in the cosmos. In order to stay with the object of his administration, he travels the path from the cosmos to humanity. He has been on this path since the eighth century, but has only really taken over his earthly office, into which his cosmic office has been transformed, in the last third of the nineteenth century.

Michael cannot force man to do anything. Force has ended due to the fact that intelligence has completely entered the domain of human individuality. But as a majestic exemplary deed in the super-sensible world, initially at the frontier of the visible world, Michael can unfold what he wishes. With a light-aura, with a spiritual gesture, Michael can show himself there, in whom all the brilliance and grandeur of the past divine intelligence is manifest. He can make visible how the effect of that past intelligence is truer, more beautiful and virtuous that the present intelligence, which streams in from Ahriman in deceptive, seductive brilliance. He can show that — *for him* — Ahriman will always be the inferior spirit under his feet.

Those who view the super-sensible world, which is at the frontier of the visible world, perceive, as here described, what Michael and his collaborators wish to do for humanity. Such people see how man is to be led in freedom through Michael's image in the Ahrimanic sphere from Ahriman to Christ. If by means of their vision such people are able to open other people's hearts and minds, in order that a circle of people know that Michael now lives among men, then humanity will begin to celebrate Michael festivals with the right contents, during which Michael's force will revive in their souls. Michael will then work as a real power among men. Man will however be *free* — and will nevertheless follow his spiritual life-path through the cosmos in inner community with Christ.

Goetheanum, October 19, 1924

109. To become really conscious of Michael's activities in his spiritual relationship to the world means to resolve the riddle of human freedom being severed from its cosmic connection, considering that the severance is necessary for earthly humanity.

110. Because the fact of "freedom" is directly given to every person who understands himself in the present stage of human evolution, no one may say, if he doesn't want to deny an obvious fact, that "there is no freedom". But one can find a contradiction between what is factually given and cosmic processes. Considering Michael's mission in the cosmos, this contradiction disappears.

111. In my "Philosophy of Freedom", one finds contemporary human "freedom" proven as a content of consciousness; in what is given here, one finds the development of this freedom cosmically substantiated.

The Future of Humanity and Michael's Activity

At this stage of his evolution, what is man's relation to Michael and his collaborators?

Man stands within a world which was once totally of divine-spiritual essence, to which he also belonged. At that time the world to which man belonged was divine-spiritual *being.* During a following stage of evolution this was no longer the case. Then it was the cosmic *revelation* of the divine-spiritual, and its being hovered behind this revelation. But it was in motion and lived in that revelation. A star-world already existed. The divine-spiritual lived in its brilliance and motion *as revelation.* One can say: where a star stood or moved, the activity of the divine-spiritual could be seen.

In all this: how the divine spirit worked in the cosmos, how man's life was a result of a divine-spiritual act in the cosmos — Michael was there, unopposed in his own element. He mediated the relationship of the divine to humanity.

Other times came. The star-world no longer directly contained divine-spiritual activity. It lived and moved persisting in the continuation of what it had previously contained. The divine-spiritual no longer lived in the cosmos as revelation, but now only as the effectiveness of its acts. A clear differentiation appeared between the divine-spiritual and what was cosmic. Michael, because of his own nature, remained with the divine-spiritual. He tried to keep humanity as close as possible to this element. He has continued to do so. He wanted to protect humanity from living too intensely in a world which is only the effect of the divine-spiritual, but not its being, and not revelation.

Michael finds it deeply satisfying that he has been able, *through humanity*, to keep the star-world directly united with the divine-spiritual in the following way. When a human being, once he has completed the life between death and a rebirth, again treads the path towards a new earthly existence, he *seeks* to create a certain harmony between the star patterns and his earthly life as he descends to this existence. This harmony was self-evidently present in older times because the divine-spiritual was active in the stars, in which human life also had its source. Today though, when the movement of the stars merely continues the *effects* of divine-spiritual activity, it will not be there if man does not seek it. Man brings the divine-spiritual elements he has retained from older times into a relation with the stars, which themselves contain only the aftereffects of the past. Thus a divine element enters into man's relation to the world which corresponds to earlier times, yet *emerges* in later times. *That this is so is Michael's deed.* And this deed gives him such deep satisfaction that a part of his life-element, his life-energy, his living sun-filled will is contained in this satisfaction.

But today, when he directs his spiritual eye towards the earth, he sees a quite different situation. During his life in the physical realm between birth and death, man is immersed in a world which no longer shows the effects of the divine-spiritual, but only what remains of these effects; one can say that what remains is only the divine-spiritual's *works*. These *works* are completely divine-spiritual in their forms. The divine shows itself to human vision in the form of natural phenomena; but it is *no longer* an enlivening element in these phenomena. Nature is a divine work and is everywhere a reflection of divine activity.

Man lives in this sun-filled divine, but not actively living divine world. However, as a result of Michael's effect on him, he has retained his connection with the essence of the divine-spiritual. He lives as a being who is permeated by God in a world which is not permeated by God.

To this God-vacated world man will bring what is in him — what *his* being has become in the present age.

Humanity will continue to develop in the evolution of the world. The divine-spiritual from which humanity originates can radiate through the cosmos — which only exists at present in the image of the divine-spiritual — as a cosmically proliferating humanity.

The being which was once cosmos will no longer be the one which now radiates through humanity. In its progression through humanity, the divine-spiritual will experience a being which it had not previously revealed.

The Ahrimanic powers are opposed to this evolutionary progression. They do not want the original divine-spiritual powers to illumine the universe in its progression; they want the cosmic intellectuality which they have absorbed to radiate through the entire new cosmos and that humanity continue to live in this intellectualized ahrimanic cosmos.

By living in this way man would lose Christ. For he has entered the world with an intellectuality which once existed totally in the divine-spiritual, when it was still, in its *essence,* shaping the cosmos. If we speak today in a way that makes our thoughts also those of Christ, we place something in opposition to the Ahrimanic powers that protects us from succumbing to them.

To understand the sense of the Michael-mission in the cosmos means to speak in this way. One must be able to speak today about nature as the Consciousness Soul evolutionary stage demands. One must absorb the purely natural scientific way of thinking. But one should also learn to speak *about nature* — meaning *to feel* — in a way which is appropriate to Christ. We should not learn the Christ-language merely about the redemption of nature, not merely about souls and divinity, but about the cosmos.

We will be able to maintain our connection with the primordial divine-spiritual and understand how to cultivate the Christ-language about the cosmos, if we completely, with all our hearts, adjust ourselves to the acts of Michael and his collaborators among us. For to understand Michael means to find the way to the logos, the Christ who lives on earth among men.

Anthroposophy correctly values what the natural scientific way of thinking has learned about the world over the past four to five hundred years, and speaks of it. But it also speaks about the nature of man, about the evolution of man and the cosmos; anthroposophy wishes to speak the language of Christ-Michael.

Both languages will then be spoken and evolution will not be defeated and succumb to the Ahrimanic before finding the divine-spiritual. To speak merely in the natural-scientific way corresponds to the separation of intellectuality from the original divine-spiritual. It *can* succumb to the Ahrimanic if Michael's mission is ignored. It will *not* succumb if the liberated intellect rediscovers itself through the force of Michael's example in the primordial cosmic intellectuality, which lies at the source of humanity and has appeared within the human domain through Christ after it abandoned man in order that his freedom could be realized.

Goetheanum, October 25, 1924

112. The divine-spiritual takes effect in the cosmos in various ways in the following stages:

    1. through its own primordial *essence;*

    2. through the *revelation* of this essence;

    3. through its *effects,* when the essence retreats from the revelation.

    4. through the *work,* when the divine is no longer in the visible universe, but only its forms.

113. In the contemporary view of nature, man has no relation to the divine, but only to its effects.

114. Michael constantly strives to embody human-cosmic evolution by being a freely active example of the divine essence and the revelatory relation to the cosmos retained by humanity from ancient times in order that what the image, the form of what the divine says about nature, may flow into a higher, spiritual consideration of nature. Although this will certainly be present in man, it will nevertheless be a reminiscence of the divine relation to the cosmos during the first two stages of cosmic evolution. In this way anthroposophy affirms the view of nature corresponding to the Consciousness-Soul age; it also completes it however, with what the eye of the spirit reveals.

Humanity's Michael-Christ-Experience

By absorbing Michael's nature and deeds with deep feeling and inner vision, one will have a correct understanding of how to grasp a world which is neither of a divine nature nor of revelation nor of effectiveness, but is the *handiwork* of the gods. To see into this world knowledgably means to have forms, formations before us which everywhere speak aloud of the divine; in which, however, if one does not succumb to illusion, no living divine being will be found. And it is not sufficient to merely consider knowledge of the world. This reveals most clearly the world's configuration which today surrounds man of course. But more important for daily life is feeling, willing, working in a world which, although seemingly divine in its formation, cannot be experienced as divinely enlivened. In order to bring true moral life into this world, the ethical impulses which I described in "The Philosophy of Freedom" are necessary.

In this *handiwork-world,* Michael's Being and contemporary deeds can be illuminating for truly feeling people. Michael does not come into the physical world phenomenally. He and all his activity remain within a super-sensible region which, however, borders on the physical world of the present phase of evolution. Therefore the possibility can never arise that the impressions that people receive through Michael cause their vision of nature to become fantastic, or that they will want to practice ethics in a god-formed but not god-enlivened world as though impulses could exist which must not be ethically-spiritually sustained by people themselves. Man will always have to approach Michael, whether by thought or volition, when moving to the spirit.

One may therefore live spiritually in the following way. Accept cognition and life as they must be accepted since the fifteenth century. But hold to the Michael-revelation, allowing it to burn brightly in thoughts that one receives from nature, carrying them as warmth in the heart when living in a world made possible by divine handiwork. One will then *not* only observe and experience the contemporary world, but also what Michael imparts — a past stage of the world, a stage which Michael carries into the present by his being and his deeds.

If it were otherwise and Michael brought his deeds into a world which man must recognize and experience as physical, then we would see in the world not what *is* in it, but what *was*. If this were to happen, then this illusory understanding of the world would deflect the reality which is appropriate for the soul to another, namely to a luciferic one.

The way in which Michael brings the past to effectiveness in the present life of humanity is coherent with the correct spiritual progress of the world which contains no luciferic elements. It is important to realize that in Michael's mission all luciferic elements will be avoided.

To realize this about the dawning Michael-Light in human history also means being able to find the correct path to Christ. Michael will give the correct orientation in respect to the world which surrounds man in order for him to know and act in it. He will have to find the way to Christ within himself.

It is completely understandable that in a time in which natural science has taken on the form which the past five hundred years have given it, that knowledge of the supersensible world has become what is currently experienced by humanity.

Nature must be known and experienced as devoid of gods. Thereby man no longer experiences himself in his relation to a world of this kind. Inasmuch as man is a supersensible being his relationship to nature, which is appropriate to the times, tells him *nothing* about his own being, nor can he live ethically in a way appropriate to his humanity.

As a result, this knowledge and way of life is induced to regard the super-sensible human being or even the super-sensible world itself as meaningless. This domain becomes separated from what is accessible to human knowledge. The separate domain of revelation by faith is ordained in contrast to what is knowable.

The purely spiritual activity of Christ, however, is in contrast to this. Since the Mystery of Golgotha Christ is accessible to the human soul. And its relation to him need not remain an undefined, dimly felt mystical one; it can be completely concrete, humanly profound and clearly experienced.

Through living together with Christ, what the human soul should know about its own super-sensible being flows into it. The revelations of faith must then be felt so that they continuously flow into the Christ experience. Thereby life will be penetrated with Christ, so that in Christ the Being is found through whom man's soul is made aware of its own super-sensible nature.

Thus the Michael experience and the Christ experience will be simultaneous. Through Michael man will be able to correctly find the way to the super-sensible in respect to exterior nature. Without falsifying it, he will view nature together with a spiritual view of the world and man, inasmuch as he is a cosmic being.

By means of the correct attitude towards Christ and active contact with Him, man will experience what he otherwise could only receive through the traditional revelation by faith. The inner world of the soul's experiences will be illumined by the spirit, as the outer world of nature is supported by the spirit.

Were man to wish to obtain information about his own super-sensible nature without living together with Christ, it would lead him out of his own reality and into that of Ahriman. Christ carries within him the impulse of the future of humanity in a valid manner. To unite with Him signifies validly receiving the seeds of the future into the human soul. Other beings, who are already showing forms which will only be cosmically valid for humanity in the future, belong to the Ahrimanic spheres. To bond with Christ in the correct way also means to protect oneself from the Ahrimanic in the correct way.

Those who strictly demand the protection of revelation by faith as opposed to the influence of human knowledge, unconsciously fear that man could thus be subjected to Ahrimanic influences. This must be understood. But it should *also* be understood that it is to the honor and true recognition of Christ when the grace-filled flow of the spirit into the human soul is attributed to the experiencing of Christ.

Thus in the future the Michael-experience and the Christ-experience can stand side by side. And man will find be able to find his way to freedom between the Luciferic illusions in thinking and life and the Ahrimanic temptation of future modes, which satisfy his pride, but do not yet correspond to *his* contemporary reality.

To succumb to Luciferic illusions means not being fully human, not wanting to advance to the stage of freedom, but to remain at a previous stage of development — as godly. To succumb to Ahrimanic temptation means not wanting to wait until at a certain stage of human development the right cosmic moment comes, but to want to anticipate this moment.

In the future Michael-Christ will stand as the signpost-word at the beginning of the path upon which man can arrive in equilibrium at his cosmic goal between the Luciferic and the Ahrimanic powers.

Goetheanum, November 2, 1924

115. Man goes his way through the cosmos in such a manner that his backward glance at the past can be falsified by luciferic impulses and his contemplations into the future deceived by ahrimanic temptations.

116. Man finds the correct antidote to luciferic falsifications by permeating his sense of knowledge and life with Michael's being and mission.

117. By doing so, man also protects himself from ahrimanic temptations, for the spiritual path to exterior nature, which is stimulated by Michael, leads to the correct attitude towards the Ahrimanic, for thereby the correct experience of Christ will be found.

Michael's Mission in the Cosmic Age of Human Freedom

When experiencing Michael's activities in the present, one is able to shed light on the cosmic nature of *freedom* through spiritual science.

This does not apply to my "Philosophy of Freedom", which refers to the purely human force of knowledge when it is related to the spiritual field. One needs, then, to recognize that this means to not yet accompany beings of other worlds. One could also say, however, that the "Philosophy of Freedom" paves the way to recognition of what can be experienced by spiritually accompanying Michael in freedom.

And that is the following.

If freedom is really to exist in human actions, what is accomplished in its light should on no account depend upon the human physical and etheric organization. What is "free" can only originate in the "I"; and the astral body must be able to vibrate with the free activity of the "I" in order to be able to transmit it to the physical and etheric bodies. But that is only one side of the matter. The other side will become clear in connection with Michael's mission.

What man experiences in freedom may not affect his etheric or physical bodies. If that happened, he would forfeit what he has become during the stage of his evolution under the influence of divine-spiritual essence and divine-spiritual *revelation*.

What man thus experiences, which is only the divine-spiritual activity *in his environment,* may only have an effect on his spirit (his I). The influence on his physical and etheric organization can only be what enters the stream of evolution not in his environment but within his being itself, and which originated in the essence and revelation of divine spirituality. It may not, however, be enmeshed with what lives in the element of freedom.

This is only possible when Michael brings from the primeval past of evolution something which gives man a relation to divine spirituality and which at present no longer intervenes in physical and etheric creation. In this way, as part of Michael's mission, the foundation for man's intercourse with the spiritual world is developed, one which does not affect the natural elements.

It is inspiring to observe how through Michael the human being is elevated to the spiritual spheres, whereas the unconscious, the subconscious, which develop below the sphere of freedom, grow closer and closer to matter.

Man's position with respect to the universe will be more distant and incomprehensible if in addition to his relationship to nature and its processes he does not also recognize ones such as Michael's mission. He gets to know his relationship to nature as something observed from without; that to the spiritual world is like having an inner conversation with beings to whom one has gained access by means of a spiritual observation of the world.

Therefore, in order to realize the impulse for freedom, man must be able to repress certain natural effects on his being that come from the cosmos. This repression takes place in the subconscious when the forces of the I's freedom come into play. Acting in freedom exists in humanity's inner perception; for the spiritual beings from other cosmic spheres who are bonded with man it is otherwise. The beings of the hierarchy of angels, who are concerned with the continuance of the human being from earth-life to earth-life, immediately see human activity in freedom thus: man repels the cosmic forces which desire to educate him further and to give his I-organization the necessary physical support, which they gave him before the age of Michael.

As a being from the hierarchy of archangels, Michael receives his impressions with help from the hierarchy of angels. He dedicates himself to the task of providing man, in the manner here described, with forces from the spiritual part of the cosmos, which can substitute for the repressed forces of nature. He accomplishes this by acting in perfect unison with the Mystery of Golgotha.

In Christ's activity within the earth's evolution lie the forces that man needs when working through freedom to compensate for the repressed impulses of nature. But then man must really bring his soul into inner community with Christ — about which we have already referred here in these Guidelines in respect to Michael's mission.

Man knows himself to be in a reality when he faces the physical sun and receives warmth and light from it.

In the same way, he must face the spiritual sun, Christ, who has united his being with the earth's being, and from that spiritual sun receive into his soul the warmth and light which corresponds to the spiritual world.

He will feel himself permeated by this "spiritual warmth" when he experiences "Christ in me". He will say to himself when feeling this permeation: "This warmth frees your humanity from cosmic bonds in which it may not remain. In order for you to achieve freedom, the divine-spiritual Being of primeval times had to lead you to regions in which it could no longer stand by you, in which it however gave you the Christ, so he could lend you his force as a free person — something the divine-spiritual Being of primeval times once gave you through the path of nature, which was then also the path of the spirit. This warmth leads you back to the divinity from which you originated."

And in feeling this with inner warmth of soul, man will experience the growing togetherness with Christ and that of real and true humanity. "Christ gives me my humanity" will be the fundamental feeling that penetrates and permeates the soul. And it is once *this* feeling exists that another also comes through which man feels himself carried up beyond mere earthly existence and feels himself as one with the stellar surroundings of the earth and with all that in this stellar environment is recognized as divine spirituality.

This also applies to the spiritual light. Man can feel himself to be completely human when he is aware of himself as a free individual. However, a darkening is associated with this. The divine spirituality of primeval times no longer shines. In the light which Christ brings to the human I the primeval light is again present. In such togetherness with Christ, this blessed thought can shine on the soul like a sun: The glorious primal divine light is here again; it shines, although its shining is not from nature. And man in the contemporary world unites himself with the spiritual cosmic shining force of the past, in which he was not yet a free individual. And in *this* light he can find the paths which rightly lead his humanity, if he understandingly unites in his soul with Michael's mission.

Then in spiritual warmth man will feel the impulse which carries him to his cosmic future in such a way that he can remain true to the primal gifts of the divine-spiritual beings, although he has developed into a free individual in their worlds. And in the spiritual light perceiving, he will feel the strength that endows him with an ever increasingly expanding consciousness and leads him to a world in which as a free human being he re-encounters the gods of his genesis.

To persist in the original naive divine grace at work in man and fearfully shun full freedom in this contemporary world where everything is disposed towards freedom, only leads man to Lucifer, who wants to see the contemporary world denied.

To gives oneself over to a contemporary world which only recognizes the natural world revealed by intellectuality and is neutral in respect to grace, and only wants to experience and use freedom intellectually, (but, however, in which evolution in deeper regions of the soul must continue and in higher ones freedom reign), leads to Ahriman, who wants to see the contemporary world completely transformed into a cosmos of intellectuality.

In such regions, in which man's gaze at the outer world is spiritually directed towards Michael, and his gaze directed towards the interior of the soul falls spiritually on Christ, thrives that soul and spiritual certainty through which he can make his way, without the loss of his origins, on the cosmic path to finding the true realization of his future.

Goetheanum, November 2, 1924

118. A free act can only be one in which no natural process plays a role, whether within man or outside him.

119. The polar contrast to this is that a natural process is suppressed in an individual's free act, which would be present in the case of an unfree act, and would give the human being his cosmically preordained state.

120. This state, in which man lives in the present and future evolutionary stages of the world, does *not* come to him through nature, but on the spiritual path by his bonding with Michael, whereby he also finds the path to Christ.

The Cosmic Thoughts in Michael's Activity and in Ahriman's

The observer of the relationship between Michael and Ahriman may well feel impelled to ask the question: How do these two spiritual powers behave in the cosmic context in as far as they are both concerned with the development of intellectual forces?

In the past Michael developed intellectuality throughout the cosmos. He did this as a servant of the divine-spiritual powers, which had given him, as well as human beings, their genesis. And he intends to maintain this relationship to intellectuality. When it was released from the divine-spiritual powers in order to find its way within human beings, Michael decided that from then on he would be in contact with humanity in the right way in order to find his own relationship to intellectuality. But he only wanted to do this by continuing as the servant of the divine-spiritual powers, the powers to whom he and man have been united since their origins. Therefore his intention is that in the future intellectuality will stream through the hearts of men, but as the same force which streamed out of the divine-spiritual powers at the beginning.

It is a completely different situation with Ahriman. He has long since separated himself from the evolutionary stream to which the aforementioned divine-spiritual powers belong. In the primeval past he placed himself alongside them as an independent cosmic power. Although he exists spatially in the world to which man belongs at present, he develops no relationship of forces with the beings who rightfully belong to this world. Only because intellectuality has been separated from the divine-spiritual essence and approaches this world does Ahriman finds himself so related to this intellectuality that he is able, in his own way, to connect through it to humanity. For what humanity receives at present as a gift, he absorbed in the primordial past. If he is able, Ahriman will make humanity's received intellect similar to his own; that is his intention.

Ahriman appropriated intellectuality at a time when he could not interiorize it. It has remained a force within his being that has nothing to do with heart and soul. Intellectuality streams out of Ahriman as a frost-bitten, soulless cosmic impulse. And *those* people who are seized by this impulse develop a logic devoid of compassion and love, which seems to speak for itself — in truth it is Ahriman speaking in it — in which there is no sign of the true, inner, loving relationship between what man is and what he thinks, speaks, does.

But Michael never appropriated intellectuality to *himself*. He manages it as a divine-spiritual force in that he feels himself united with the divine-spiritual powers. By thus permeating intellectuality, he indicates the potentiality in it to be just as valid an expression of the heart, the soul, as of the head, the spirit. For Michael carries within him all the primal forces of his gods and those of man. Thereby he does not transfuse intellectuality with wintry frost devoid of soul, but he stands by it in soul-filled inner warmth.

This is also the reason why Michael wanders through the cosmos with earnest mien and gesture. Inwardly *so* united with intelligent content as he is means that he must also fulfill the condition not to introduce anything of subjective arbitrariness, wishes or desire into this content. Otherwise logic would be the arbitrariness of *one* being instead of an expression of the cosmos. To maintain his being as an expression of the cosmic essence; to leave everything in his inner self which reflects his own being — Michael considers this to be *his* virtue. His significance is directed towards the great context of the cosmos — his mien expresses this; his will, which approaches man, is meant to reflect what he perceives in the cosmos. His bearing and his gestures express this. Michael is earnest in everything, for earnestness as the revelation of a being is the mirror of the cosmos from that being; Smiling is the expression of what streams into the world from a being.

One of the *Michaelic* imaginations is the following: He moves with the *flow of time,* borne by cosmic light as his essence; framing cosmic warmth as the revealer of his own being; A being akin to a world, he wanders in waves affirming himself in that he affirms the world, leading forces from all corners of the universe down to earth.

In contrast an *Ahrimanic* one: In his progress he would conquer space from time, he is surrounded by darkness in which he send the rays of his own light; the more he achieves his goal, stronger is the frost around him; he moves as a world which is completely concentrated in one being, his own, in which he only affirms himself by denying the world; he moves as though he carried with him the sinister forces of earth's dark caves.

If man seeks freedom without detouring into egotism, when freedom becomes the pure love of action, then it is possible for him to approach Michael; if he wishes to act in freedom by developing egotism, if freedom is the *prideful* desire to reveal *himself* in his acts, then he is in danger of falling into Ahriman's realm.

The imaginations described above beam forth man's love for action (Michael) or his self-love when he acts (Ahriman).

In that man feels himself as a free being to be near to Michael, he is on the way to carry the force of intellectuality into his "whole humanity"; although he thinks with his head, his heart fills his thinking with either light or darkness; his will streams from his humanity in that his thoughts stream into him as intentions. The human being becomes more human when he is an expression of the world; he finds himself, not by *seeking* himself, but by willingly uniting himself with the world.

If man succumbs to Ahriman's temptations while developing his freedom, he will be dragged into intellectuality like a spiritual automaton, in which he is a cog, but no longer *himself*. All his thinking is a function of the head; this alone separates it from the experiences of the heart and his own will and snuffs out his individuality. Man loses more and more of his inner humanity by becoming the expression of his own individuality; he loses himself by *seeking* himself. He withdraws from the world to which he denies love; but man only truly experiences himself if he loves the world.

It is perhaps obvious from the forgoing that Michael is the guide to Christ. Michael travels with love through the world with all the earnestness of his being, his posture and his acts. Whoever adheres to him cultivates love *in relation to the outer world.* And love in relation to the outer world must first be developed, otherwise it is selflove.

If this love in the Michaelic sense exists, then *love for the other* can also stream back to one's own self. One will be able to love without loving one's self. And on the path of such love Christ is to be found by the human soul. Whoever adheres to Michael cultivates love in relation to the outer world, and thereby he finds the relation to his soul's inner world, which leads him to Christ.

The age now dawning requires that humanity view a spiritual world in closest proximity to the perceived physical one, and in which can be found what has been described here as the Michael-Being and the Michael-Mission. For *that* world which man envisions when perceiving *this* physical world as nature is not the one in which he directly lives, but one which is as far *beneath* the truly human one as the *Michaelic* one is *above* it. But he doesn't realize that when he makes an image of his world, another one unconsciously arises. When he paints this picture he is already in the process of alienating himself and becoming a spiritual automaton. Man can only preserve his humanity if he confronts the image of himself immersed in nature with the one in which Michael reigns, the one in which Michael leads the way to Christ.

121. One has not yet comprehended what is active in the world and the meaning for the world of these activities, for example cosmic thoughts, if one goes no farther than these activities themselves. For one must perceive the being from whom these activities originate. For example whether the cosmic thoughts are brought into and throughout the world by Michael or Ahriman.

122. What can have a wholesome and creative effect coming from one being because of his relation to the world, can be proven perverse and destructive when it comes from another being. Cosmic thoughts carry man into the future if he receives them from Michael; they lead him away from his wholesome future if Ahriman gives them to him.

123. Through such considerations one is ever more able to overcome the viewpoint of a vague spirituality, that pantheism which is thought to be the foundation of things; and one is then led to a definite, concrete viewpoint which enables him to form representations [mental pictures] of the *spiritual beings* of the higher hierarchies. For reality is present everywhere in existential being*; and what is not existential being in this reality is the activity which is acted out in the relation from being to being. This can only be understood by directing one's gaze to the active spiritual beings.

* *im Wesenhaften*

First Contemplation: How Michael prepares his earthly mission in the spiritual world by conquering Lucifer at the Gates of the Consciousness Soul

Michael's intervention in the evolution of the world and man during the end of the nineteenth century appears in a special light when one considers the spiritual history of the previous centuries.

The beginning of the fifteenth century is the age in which the consciousness soul epoch began. Before this time a complete change is evident in human spiritual life. One can follow how previously everywhere imaginations still played a significant role in human perceptions. Individual personalities had, however, already found their way to mere mental "comprehension"; but the great majority lived absorbing imaginations involving representations [mental pictures] derived exclusively from the physical world. It was so in respect to ideas about natural events as well as historical developments.

What spiritual observation finds is completely confirmed by external evidences. We will now indicate some of these.

What was thought and said about historical events in the previous centuries was often recorded just before the dawn of the Consciousness Soul age. Thus we still have the "sagas" and similar writings preserved, which give a true picture of what was then considered to be "history".

A beautiful example is the story of "Gerhard the Good", which is preserved in a poem by Rudolf von Ems, who lived in the first half of the thirteenth century. Gerhard the Good is a rich merchant in Cologne. He goes on a business trip to Russia, Livonia and Prussia to buy sable. Then he travels to Damascus and Nineveh for silk and similar things.

Homeward bound, he is thrown off course by a storm. In the strange land where he finds himself he comes to know a man who holds captive some English knights and the English king's betrothed. Gerhard gives up all he has gained on the trip in return for the captives. He takes them with him on his ship and begins the journey home. When the ship comes to the place where the routes to Gerhard's home and England separate, he lets the male prisoners leave for England, but he keeps the king's betrothed with him in the hope that King William will come to get her as soon as he learns of her liberation and where she is. The king's bride and the maidens who accompany her are kept in the very best accommodations. She lives in her liberator's house like a well-loved daughter. A long time passes without the English king coming to get her. So Gerhard decides to marry her to his son in order to ensure her future, for he thinks that William could be dead. The marriage feast is already in progress when an unknown pilgrim appears — William. He had wandered a long time on false paths seeking his betrothed. She is returned to him after Gerhard's son's selfless renunciation. They remain with Gerhard a while, who then equips a ship to take them back to England.

Once the ex-prisoners have been restored to their proper honorable station and Gerhard visits England, the English want to make *him* king. But he objects that he had delivered their rightful royal pair to them. They had also thought William dead and wanted to elect another king for the country in which conditions had become chaotic during Williams wanderings. The merchant of Cologne rejects all the honors and riches offered to him and returns to Cologne in order to be the simple merchant he was before.

The story is enhanced so that the Saxon emperor, Otto the First, travels to Cologne in order to meet "Gerhard the Good". For the powerful emperor was tempted to consider much of what he has done to be worthy of "earthly compensation". In coming to know Gerhard however, he encounters a palpable example of how a simple man does inexpressible good — giving up all the goods he has acquired to free the prisoners; returning the son's bride to William; then doing everything he can to bring the king back to England and so forth — without desiring any earthly compensation, but relying entirely on the expectation of compensation from the gods. The man is called "Gerhard the Good" by all. The emperor feels that he has received a powerful a religious-moral impulse through acquaintance with Gerhard's convictions.

The story, which I have outlined here in order not to merely mention by name something less known, clearly shows *one aspect* of the mentality of the age preceding the birth of the Consciousness Soul in human evolution. Whoever feels the spirit of this story as related by Rudolf von Ems can also sense how experience of the earthly world has changed since when Emperor Otto lived (in the tenth century).

One sees how in the Consciousness Soul age the world has become in a certain sense "clear" to the human mind as far as understanding physical being and becoming is concerned. Gerhard navigates with his ship in a virtual fog. He only knows a small piece of the world with which he wants to come into contact. In Cologne one has no knowledge of what is happening in England and it takes years to find a man who lives in Cologne. One comes to know the life and property of a man such as the one Gerhard encountered on his trip home only when he is directly brought by destiny to the corresponding location. Comparing the conditions of today with those times is like viewing the world in a wide, sun-filled landscape on one hand, and groping in dense fog on the other.

What is considered "historical" today has nothing to do with the story of "Gerhard the Good", although the latter has much to do with the mood and spiritual conditions of that age. *These*, and not specific physical events, are portrayed in imaginations. In this portrayal is shown how man does not only feel himself to be a being who lives and acts as a link in the physical chain of events, but also how in his physical existence spiritual, super-sensible beings intercede and accompany his will. The story of "Gerhard the Good" shows how man's view of the physical world through a glass darkly, which preceded the Consciousness Soul age, oriented his gaze towards the spiritual world. One did not see *in the distance* of the physical world, but one saw that much *deeper* into the spiritual one. But although a dim (dream-like) clairvoyance once showed humanity the spiritual world, it was no longer the case in that age. The imaginations were there, but they appeared in minds already strongly tending towards the theoretical. The effect was that one no longer knew how the world which manifested itself in imaginations was related to physical existence. Therefore the imaginations now appeared to more intellectual types who considered them to be arbitrary "fictions" devoid of reality.

It was no longer realized that through imaginations one saw a world in which one stands with a completely different part of his humanity than the physical one. Thus in this story both worlds stand side by side; and due to the way it is told, both worlds are characterized as if the spiritual events could have been as perceptible as the physical ones. Furthermore, in many such stories physical events were jumbled together. Persons who lived centuries apart appear as contemporaries; events are displaced to incorrect places or at incorrect times. Facts of the physical world are described in a way only appropriate for the spiritual world, for which time and space have a different meaning; the physical world is described in imaginations instead of thoughts. Therewith the spiritual world is interwoven into the story as though it did not relate to a different state of being, but to a continuation of physical facts.

Sticking to only the physical version of history, one thinks that the old imaginations of the east, Greece and so forth, had been adopted and then poetically interwoven with the physical things which people occupied themselves with at that time. They had, after all, in Isidor de Sevilla's writings from the seventh century, a proper collection of old saga motifs.

But this is an external way of understanding. It is only meaningful to those who have no idea of a human mentality which knows that its existence is still directly bound to the spiritual world and feels compelled to express this knowledge in imaginations. If instead of one's own imagination a historically documented one is used is not the essential point. This is because the soul is oriented towards the spiritual world, so that it sees both its own acts and natural events integrated in that world. Nevertheless, confusion may be noted in story-telling at the time before the dawn of the Consciousness Soul age.

Spiritual observation sees the work of luciferic forces in this confusion.

What impelled the soul to assimilate imaginations into the content of its experiences corresponded less to the capacities which it possessed in antiquity though dreamlike clairvoyance than to those that existed in the eighth to fourteenth centuries. *These* capacities impelled more to a thoughtful understanding of sense perceptions. Both capacities were present during the transitional stage. The soul was placed between the old orientation which was absorbed in the spiritual world together with the physical one which saw things as in a fog — and the new one which was absorbed in physical events and in which spiritual perceptions faded away.

Luciferic forces intruded in this oscillating equilibrium of the human soul. They wished to hinder man's finding full orientation in the physical world. They wished to keep his consciousness in the spiritual regions which were appropriate in older times. They wished to prevent pure thinking from entering into his dreamlike imaginative world-vision. They may have been able to prevent his ability to perceive the physical world correctly. They could not, however, correctly sustain the experience of the old imaginations. So they let him muse on old imaginations without being able to mindfully make the transition into the world in which imaginations are fully valid.

At the dawn of the Consciousness Soul age Lucifer acted so that through him man was transposed to the super-sensible region, which was, at first, bordering on the physical one, in a way which was inappropriate.

This can be clearly seen in the "saga" of "Herzog [Duke] Ernst", which was one of the most popular tales during the middle ages and was told everywhere.

Herzog Ernst comes into conflict with the emperor, who unjustly wants to ruin him by means of war. In order to avoid this impossible situation he takes part in the crusade to the orient. In the adventures which he experiences on the journey to his goal the physical is interwoven with the spiritual, "saga-like" in the already mentioned manner. For example, on the way the Duke encounters a people whose heads are shaped like cranes; he is shipwrecked on the "magnet mountain", the ship being attracted by its magnetic power, so that people who come close to the mountain can never get away and die a wretched death. Herzog Ernst and his people escape by sewing themselves into skins, then letting themselves be carried to another mountain by griffins, which are accustomed to scavenge for people wrecked on the magnet mountain. They then cut themselves out of the skins when the griffins aren't around and escape. Then their journey takes them to a land of people whose ears are so long that they can cover their entire bodies with them like clothing; to another people whose feet are so large that they can lie on their backs when it rains and use them as umbrellas. They come to a country of dwarfs, of giants, and so on. Such things were told about Herzog Ernst's crusade journey. Sagas do not allow a correct feeling of how wherever imaginations enter the scene an orientation towards the spiritual world occurs, where things are described through pictures which take place in the astral world and relate to human will and destiny.

And it is also the case with the beautiful "Roland-saga" in which Charlemagne's great march against the heathen in Spain is glamorized, to the extent that in order for Charlemagne to attain his goal the sun's course is delayed so that one day becomes as long as two, therewith evoking the Bible.

And in the Nibelungen saga one sees how the forms were retained in the northern lands so that spiritual perception was purer, whereas in Central Europe the imaginations were brought closer to physical life. In the northern form the story is expressed in a way that relates to an "astral world"; in the Central European form the Nibelungen song tends toward a view of the physical world.

Also the imaginations in the Herzog Ernst saga relate in reality to what is experienced *between* the happenings in the physical sphere — experienced in an "astral world", to which man belongs as well as he does to the physical one.

Observing all this with spiritual vision, one sees how entering into the Consciousness Soul age entails emerging from an evolutionary phase in which the luciferic forces would have prevailed over humanity if the Consciousness Soul with its strength of intellectuality had not introduced a new evolutionary impulse in humanity. The orientation towards the spiritual world along the path of aberration is avoided through the Consciousness Soul. The vision of humanity is withdrawn [from aberration] and guided towards the physical world. Everything that happens in this direction shields humanity from the aberrations of the luciferic forces.

From the spiritual world Michael is already actively present for humanity. From the super-sensible regions he prepares his later work. He gives humanity impulses which retain the previous relation to the divine-spiritual world, without this retention taking on a luciferic character. For in the last third of the nineteenth century Michael pressed forward in the physical world itself with the activity that he had prepared in supersensible regions from the fifteenth up until the nineteenth centuries.

Humanity had to undergo for a while a spiritual development freeing it from that relationship with the spiritual world which threatened to become an impossible one. Thereupon this development was guided, through the Michael Mission, along paths which brought the progress of earthly humanity back to a relationship with the spiritual world which is beneficial to it. Thus in his activity Michael stands between the luciferic *world-view* and the Ahrimanic *world-intelligence.* With Michael this worldview becomes a wisdom filled *world-revelation* which reveals world-intelligence as divine *world-action.* In this world-action lives Christ's wish for humanity that Michael's *world-revelation* may be unveiled to the human heart.

Goetheanum, November 23, 1924

(The second and third contemplations follow.)

Further Guidelines with reference to the previous First Contemplation about Michael's supersensible preparations for his earth mission.

124. The dawn of the age of consciousness (fifteenth century), in the twilight of the *Comprehension or Sensitivity Soul age*, was preceded by intense luciferic activity, which still continues for a time in the new epoch. [The italicized words have almost always been translated as "Intellectual or Mind Soul age". I believe this is a mistranslation and have therefore used the

more accurate "Comprehension or Sensitivity Soul age" wherever it appears. Trans.]

125. The intent of this luciferic activity is to wrongfully retain the old forms of image-thinking of the world and thus prevent man from understanding and integrating himself into its physical nature.

126. Michael associates with human activity in order that independent intellectuality remain correctly connected to the divine spirituality from which it descended.

Second Contemplation: How the Michael Forces functioned during the first unfolding of the Consciousness Soul

At the time of the dawn of the Consciousness Soul in man's earthly evolution, it was difficult for the beings from the spiritual region closest to the earth to approach humanity. Earthly events acquired a form which showed that relations of a very special kind were necessary for spirituality to make its way into the physical life of man. But on the other hand, that form also shows in an often most clarifying manner how where spiritual powers of the past are *still* active and the powers of the future *already* begin to be active, one spiritual entity energetically seeks its way into humanity's earthy life in opposition to the other.

Between 1339 and 1453 France and England were engaged in a senseless war for over a hundred years. These spiritually chaotic events, unfavorable for human development, were responsible for delaying the introduction of the Consciousness Soul, which would have appeared sooner had those events not occurred. *Chaucer,* who died in 1400, laid the foundation for English literature. One needs only to consider the spiritual consequences for Europe of this foundation and one will find it meaningful that it could not develop freely, but succumbed to the confusion of war. Furthermore, already earlier (1215) the political thinking characteristic of the Consciousness Soul had begun to take shape in England. The further development of this event was also hindered by the chaos of war.

This was a time when the spiritual forces wanting man to develop as he had been disposed from the beginning by the divine-spiritual forces above them met their adversaries. These adversaries wished to detour man onto roads other than those meant for him from the beginning. He would then not be able to use the forces of his origin for his subsequent evolution. His cosmic childhood would thus remain unfruitful. It would be like a fading part of his being. The result would be that man could become prey to the Luciferic or Ahrimanic powers and his individual development would fall short. If the efforts of these anti-human adversarial powers had been completely successful instead of merely being a hindering factor, the introduction of the Consciousness Soul could have been completely prevented.

An event which illustrates especially well the streaming of spirituality into earthly events was the emergence and destiny of Jeanne d'Arc, the maid of Orleans (14121431). What she did came from the deepest subconscious fount of her soul. She followed the faint inspirations of the spiritual world. Chaos reigned on earth, through which the Consciousness Soul age was to be hindered. Michael had to prepare his future mission from the spiritual world. He was only able to do so when his impulses were received by human souls. The maid of Orleans had such a soul. He also acted through many other souls, even when it was only possible in a moderate way and is less apparent to official history. He met his Ahrimanic adversary in such events as the war between England and France.

The Luciferic adversary he met in those times was spoken of in the previous contemplation. But the events show that that adversary was also especially active in the time following the Maid of Orleans appearance. One sees in those events that humanity was unable to contend with the intervention of the spirit-world in human affairs, which was understood and could also be integrated into the will at a time when imaginative understanding was still present. Contention with such intervention became impossible with the end of the Comprehension or Sensitivity Soul era; the attitude corresponding to the Consciousness Soul had not yet been found at that time; it has not yet been accomplished even today.

What happened was that Europe's formation was arranged from the spiritual world, without man realizing what was happening and without his efforts having a meaningful influence.

To appreciate the meaning of those events, which were realized from the spirit world, one needs only to imagine what would have happened in the fifteenth century if there had been no Maid of Orleans,. There are also people who try to explain such occurrences materialistically. Making them understand is impossible, because they arbitrarily give a materialistic meaning to what is obviously spiritual.

This clearly shows that humanity's striving to find the path to divine spirituality was no longer without difficulties, even when it was intensively sought. Such difficulties did not exist in the age when insight could be obtained by means of imaginations. In order to correctly judge what is meant, it is only necessary to clearly observe the persons who had emerged as philosophers. A philosopher cannot be judged only by his effect on his times, nor how many people have taken up his ideas. He is much more the *expression,* the personification of his times. What the majority of people already experience as unconscious feelings and motives are introduced by the philosopher with his ideas. He indicates the mentality of his times as a thermometer indicates the temperature of its surroundings. Philosophers are as little the cause of the mentality of their times as the thermometer is of the temperature of its surroundings.

In this respect, consider the philosopher *Rene Descartes* (1596-1650), who was active when the consciousness soul age was already in progress. The thin thread of his connection with the spirit world (true being) was his experience of "I think, therefore I am". In the center of the Consciousness Soul, the I, he tried to experience reality; and only to the extent of what the Consciousness Soul could tell him.

And he sought clarity about the rest of spirituality by intellectually investigating how much guarantee the certainty of his own self-awareness provided for the certainly of other things. He asked everywhere about the truths which had been handed down historically: are they as clear as "I think, therefore I am"? If he can affirm this, he accepts them. Doesn't this kind of thinking directed towards the things of the world ignore the spirit? This spirit's revelation had restricted itself to the thinnest thread in self-awareness; everything else showed itself to be directly revealed without spiritual revelation. What lies beyond self-awareness can only indirectly throw a flicker of light of this spiritual revelation into the Consciousness Soul through the intellect. The person of that time let his still relatively empty-of-content Consciousness Soul strive with intense desire towards the spiritual world. A thin stream gets there.

The beings of the spirit-world directly bordering on the earth, and the human souls on earth, came together with difficulty. Michael's super-sensible preparations for his later mission were experienced by human souls only with the greatest inhibitions.

We may compare, in order to understand the different mentalities, the ideas expressed by Descartes and Augustine, the latter possessing the same slim foundation for experiencing the spiritual world as Descartes — at least in respect to his formulations. Except that in Augustine's case it derived from the full imaginative force of the Comprehension or Sensitivity Soul. (He lived from 354 to 430.) Augustine and Descartes are considered to be related — and correctly so. However, Augustine's intellect was still a vestige of the cosmos, whereas Descartes' intellect had been absorbed into the individual human soul. One can see from the process of spiritual striving from Augustine to Descartes how the cosmic character of thinking power is lost, and then appears again in the human soul. At the same time one can also see how Michael and human minds come together under difficult conditions, so that Michael can guide them, as he once did in the cosmos.

The Luciferic and Ahrimanic forces are at work to obstruct this coordination. The Luciferic forces want man to develop only what was appropriate to his cosmic infancy. The Ahrimanic ones, in opposition but simultaneously collaborating, would like to see only the forces to be developed during a later epoch flourish, and let the cosmic infancy fade out.

Against such increasing opposition, the human souls of Europe processed the spiritual impulses of the old worldview ideas streaming from the East to the West through the Crusades. The Michael forces lived strongly in those ideas. Cosmic intelligence, the direction of which was Michael's ancient spiritual heritage, dominated these worldviews.

How could they be absorbed when a chasm existed between the forces of the spirit-world and human souls? They entered into the slowly evolving Consciousness Soul. On one side, they encountered the obstacle which still existed in the weakly developed Consciousness Soul, which lamed them. On the other side, they no longer possessed an imaginative consciousness. Human souls could no longer connect to them with insight. They were received either superficially or superstitiously.

Names such as Wicliff, Huss and others on one hand, and the term "Rosicrucian" on the other, should be understood with this mentality in mind.

Goetheanum, November 30, 1924

We will speak of this further.

(The continuation of this second contemplation and the third will follow.)

127. At the beginning of the Consciousness Soul age human souls had still only developed their intellectual forces to a limited degree. There was a lack of coherence between what these souls desired in the depths of their unconscious and what forces from the region where Michael was could give them.

128. In this lack of coherence a spiritual opportunity existed for the Luciferic powers to hold back humanity at its cosmic childhood, and not permit it to develop further on the divine spiritual paths with which it was united from the beginning, but on Luciferic ones.

129. Furthermore, the spiritual opportunity existed for the Ahrimanic powers to completely disconnect humanity from its cosmic childhood and thus absorb it into their own realm in future evolution.

130. Neither of these things happened, because the Michael-forces *were* active; but human spiritual development had to take place under the hindrances caused by these opportunities, and became what it is now *because* of them.

Continuation of the Second Contemplation: Hindrance and Furtherance of the Michael Forces at the Dawn of the Conscious Soul Age

In all of Europe the incorporation of the consciousness soul also had the effect of disturbing religious faith and the experience of ritual. At the turn of the eleventh and twelfth centuries one sees the advance notices of this disturbance in the appearance of the "proofs of God" (especially by Anselm of Canterbury). The existence of God was to be proven through reason. Such a desire could only appear when the old way, to experience "God" with the soul's forces, was disappearing. For what one experiences in that way cannot be proven logically.

The previous way was for the soul to perceive the intelligent beings — up to the Godhead; the new way became to form thoughts intellectually about the "primal ground" of the universe. The first way was supported by the forces of Michael in the spiritual regions at the periphery of the earth, which equipped the soul with capacities beyond the forces of sense-thinking to perceive the intelligent beings in the universe; for the second way the soul's connection with the Michael-forces first had to be accomplished.

Extensive areas of human religious life, such as the central teaching of Holy Communion, began to falter — through Wicliff in England (fifteenth century) to Huss in Bohemia. In Holy Communion man could find his connection to the spirit-world, which was opened to him by Christ, for he was able to unite his being with Christ in such a way that the fact of union through the senses was at the same time a spiritual one.

The consciousness of the Comprehension or Sensitivity Soul was able to understand this union. For this soul could still conceive of the spirit as well as of matter, which were so close that the transition of the one (matter) into the other (spirit), was conceivable. Such ideas should not be so intellectual that they require proof of God's existence; they must be ideas which still have something of imagination. Thereby the active spirit in matter is felt, and in the spirit the striving for matter. Behind ideas of *this* kind are Michael's cosmic forces.

Just consider how much faltered for the human soul during that time! How much of what was related to its most inner and holiest experience! Personalities such as Huss, Wicliff and others appeared, in whom the Consciousness Soul shone brightest, whose soul constitutions strongly united them with the Michael-forces, something which would happen to others centuries later. They asserted the Consciousness Soul's right to vibrantly grasp the religious mysteries. They felt: intellectuality, which arose together with the Consciousness Soul, must be capable of including in its ideas what was achieved through imagination in older times.

On the other hand, the human soul's old traditional attitude had lost all its inner strength in the widest circles. What is historically called abuses of the religious life, with which the great reformation councils occupied themselves at the time of the beginning of Consciousness Soul's activity, is all related to the lives of those who did not yet feel the Consciousness Soul within them, but could no longer find something which could give them inner strength and certainty in the Comprehension or Sensitivity Soul.

One can truly say that such historical human experiences as came about in the councils of Constance and Basel illustrate the streaming down of intellectuality towards humanity from the spirit world above — and below the earthly region with a no-longer-suitable Comprehension or Sensitivity Soul. In between the Michael-forces oscillated, looking back at their previous connection to divine spirituality and downward at humanity, which also had that connection, but which now had to move to a sphere in which Michael would have to help spiritually, although he was not yet able to inwardly unite with that sphere. In Michael's efforts, which are *necessary* in cosmic evolution, but which nevertheless are at first a disturbance of the equilibrium in the cosmos, is also the reason for what humanity experienced at that time in regard to the holiest truths.

One looks deeply into the characteristics of that age by studying Cardinal Nicolaus Cusanus. (See references to him in my book

Mysticism and Modern Thought.) His personality is like a signpost of the times. He wanted to enforce viewpoints which would not combat the physical world's evils with fanatical tendencies, but with common sense — to get the train of thought back on track. His actions at the Council of Basel and in his church parish are evidence of this.

Nicolaus tended completely toward the evolutionary transition to the Consciousness Soul, and on the other hand he revealed viewpoints which indicate the forces of Michael in shining armor. He included the good old ideas, those which lead human minds toward the development of capacities for the perception of intelligences in the cosmos, when Michael still directed the Universal-Intellectuality. The "learned ignorance" of which he spoke refers to what is beyond understanding through sense perception: that thinking beyond intellectuality (common knowledge) leads into a region where — unknowingly — the spiritual is grasped in living vision.

Thus Nicolaus is a person who, feeling the disturbance of cosmic equilibrium through Michael in his own soul, intuitively wanted to do everything possible to orient this disturbance towards the healing of humanity.

Something else hid between these events. Individual personalities who understood the meaning of the Michael forces in the universe wished to prepare their own souls to be able to consciously gain access to the spiritual region bordering the earthly region, where Michael was working for the benefit of humanity.

They sought justification for this spiritual undertaking by acting in their professions and otherwise in such a way that they would not be distinguishable from others. Thereby, that they carried out their earthly duties in such a loving way, they were able to freely devote their inner selves to the mentioned spiritual task. What they did in this respect were the things for which they came together "in secret". From the standpoint of what happened physically, the world was at first apparently untouched by this spiritual striving. Nevertheless, it was necessary in order to connect souls to the Michael-World. They were not "secret societies" in any negative sense, not seekers for what is hidden because it shuns the light of day. Rather were they associations of people who were convinced that their members were conscious of Michael's mission. Therefore they did not speak of their work in front of those who would only disturb their tasks due to lack of understanding. These tasks consisted at first of working in spiritual streams which did not move in earthly life, but in the neighboring spirit-world which, however, sent its spiritual impulses into earthly life.

It was a matter of the spiritual activity of people who stood in the physical world, but cooperated with Beings of the spirit-world, with Beings who did not incorporate into the physical world. They were called — not very accurately — Rosicrucian's. True Rosicrucianism was completely in line with the Michael-Mission activity. It helped Michael prepare his spiritual work on earth for what he intended for a future age.

We can judge what happened by taking the following into account. The difficulty, rather the impossibility for Michael to enter human souls was because he did not want to come in any way into contact with the contemporary physical world. He wanted to remain in the force complex that existed for spirits of his kind and for humans *in the past.* Any contact with what man *must* come into contact with in physical earthly life *could* only be considered by Michael to be a contamination of his being. In normal human life, the soul's spiritual experiences work into his physical earthly life, and the latter into the former. This reverse effect is evidenced namely in man's attitude and his orientation towards the earthly. Such intertwining effect is the rule — although not always — especially for people in public life. Therefore Michael's activities in respect to many reformers encountered strong obstacles.

The Rosicrucian's overcame these difficulties by keeping their normal lives with their earthly duties totally apart from their work with Michael. When he, with his impulses, encountered what a Rosicrucian had prepared for him in his soul, he found himself in no way exposed to the danger of earthly contact. Because what united the Rosicrucian with Michael was kept safely apart by the Rosicrucian's state of soul. This true Rosicrucian resolve forged the path to be found on earth for Michael's coming mission.

Goetheanum, December 6, 1924

(The third contemplation follows.)

Further Guidelines for the Anthroposophical Society at the Goetheanum

(With reference to the preceding two contemplations about Hindrance and Furtherance of the Michael Forces at the dawn of the Consciousness Soul age.)

131. At the beginning of the Consciousness Soul age the emancipated intellectuality in man wanted to occupy itself with truths of religion and ritual. Human soul-life experienced uncertainty, a faltering thereby. An attempt was made to prove logically what was previously experienced by the soul. The content of ritual, which must be grasped in imaginations, was to be grasped through logical conclusions — even be conducted according to them.

132. This is all related to the fact that *Michael* wanted, under all circumstances, to avoid any contact with the physical earth — upon which *man must* walk — although he was to continue to accompany the cosmic intellectuality, which he administered in the past, in humanity. Thereby through the Michael-forces a disturbance occurred in cosmic equilibrium which was *necessary* for the continuation of world evolution.

133. Michael's mission was made easier when certain personalities — the true Rosicrucians — organized their normal earthly lives in such a way that they in no way interfered with their inner soul lives. They could therefore develop forces internally through which they could cooperate with Michael spiritually without him running the danger of being enmeshed in earthly events — which would have been out of the question for him.

Third Contemplation: Michael's anxiety about human evolution before the time of his earthly activity

During the development of the Consciousness Soul age the possibility of a connection between Michael and humanity in general gradually ceased. Humanized intellectuality intervened. Imaginative ideas, which could show man the essential intelligence in the cosmos, faded away. The possibility for Michael to approach humanity only began during the last third of the nineteenth century. Previously this could only happen on the path to true Rosicrucianism.

Man looked at nature with his budding intellect. He saw there a physical and an etheric world in which he was absent. Through the great ideas of Copernicus and Galileo he acquired an image of the external world — but lost his own image. He looked at himself and had no insight into *what* he is. In the depths of his being the bearer of his intelligence — his "I" awakened. Thus man contained a triplicity. Firstly, *that* which originally placed his soul-spiritual being — as a physical-etheric entity — in the ancient

Saturn and Sun times and thereafter again and again in the domain of divine spirituality. That is where the human being and Michael could walk together. Secondly, man carried within him his later physical and etheric being, that which he became during the ancient Moon and Earth epochs. All that was the work and activity of divine spirituality — which, however, was no longer actively present.

It would only become actively present when Christ passed through the Mystery of Golgotha. Christ can be found in what works spiritually in the physical and etheric bodies of man. Thirdly, man had within him that part of his soul-spiritual being which had taken on *new* being during the ancient Moon and the earth epochs. In this being Michael remained active, whereas in the part which tended towards the ancient Moon and the earth he became less active. Within the new being *he* [Michael] preserved for man his man-god image.

He was able to do this at the dawn of the Consciousness Soul age. Then man's entire soul-spirit reality sank into the physical-etheric in order to extract the Consciousness Soul from it. Man's consciousness rose up brilliantly in respect to what his physical and etheric bodies could tell him about the physical and etheric in nature. His vision diminished, however, concerning what his astral body and his I could tell him about himself.

A time came in which man felt that he could no longer have insight about himself. A *search* for knowledge of humanity began. What the present offered did not satisfy him, so he went back in time historically. Humanism arose in cultural development. People looked towards humanism not because they knew man, but because they had *lost* him. If *Erasmus of Rotterdam* and others had known man, they would have taken quite a different approach than through what humanism meant for them.

Later in *Faust* Goethe created a human figure who had completely lost the meaning of humanity.

This search for the "human being" became more and more intense. The only choices were either to dampen one's sense of self; or to develop the desire for it as an element of the soul.

Up into the nineteenth century the best people in European culture developed ideas — historical, natural scientific, philosophical, mystical — which indicated efforts to discover the *human* within a worldview that had become intellectual.

Renaissance, spiritual rebirth, humanism hastened, even stampeded in striving for spirituality in a direction in which it was *not* to be found; and only impotence, illusion and stupefaction were found in the direction in which it must be sought. Along with this came the breakthrough of the Michael forces in man — in art, in knowledge, only not yet in the renewing forces of the Consciousness Soul — which meant instability for spiritual life. Michael was directing all his strength backward in cosmic evolution to gain the power needed to hold the "dragon" in equilibrium under his feet. It was just then during Michael's striving for power that the great renaissance creations took place. But they were a renewal by Michael of the

Comprehension or Sensitivity Soul elements, and not the result of new soul forces.

Michael was full of anxiety as to whether he would be able to do battle with the "Dragon" for very long when he saw the attempt to add an image of man similar to the one newly acquired in respect to the natural realm. Michael saw how nature was observed and how people wanted to form an image of man according to what they called "natural law". He saw how it was thought that as animal characteristics became more perfect, the organ system more harmonious, man "came into being". But it was not "man" that came into being in Michael's spiritual view, because what was thought about perfection and harmony was merely "thought"; nobody could observe that it was real because it had never happened anywhere.

And thus people lived with thoughts about man in unreal images, in illusions; they hunted for an image of man which they only thought to have found; but in reality their field of vision was empty. "The spiritual sun's force illumines their souls, Christ acts, but they cannot yet see it. Consciousness Soul forces are active with love, but not yet in souls." Inspiration can hear something like this as Michael speaks with great anxiety: What if the strength of illusion in man could give the "dragon" so much power that it would not be possible for him — Michael — to maintain the equilibrium?

Other personalities tried with artistic inner strength to experience nature at one with man. Powerful were Goethe's words when he described Winckelmann's work in a great book: "When man's healthy nature acts as a whole, when he feels himself as in a great, beautiful, majestic and worthy whole, when harmonious contentment provides him with pure, free delight; then the universe, if it could feel itself as having reached its goal, would exult and marvel at its own becoming and essence." What Lessing celebrated with passionate spirituality, what ensouled the great worldview in Herder — resounded in Goethe's words. And all of Goethe's creativity is like a many-sided manifestation of these words. In his "Aesthetic Letters" Schiller described a perfect man who, as is reflected in these words, contains the universe and realizes it in social contact with others. But from where does this image of man originate? It blazes like the morning sun over the earth in springtime. But for humanity it originated in the Greek idea of man. It was cultivated with a strong inner Michael-impulse; but people could only realize this impulse by looking back into the past. Goethe felt an extremely strong conflict with the Consciousness Soul when he tried to experience "man". He sought him in Spinoza's philosophy; but it was during his Italian journey when he looked into the Greek essence that he felt he could correctly sense him. He hurried away from the Consciousness Soul to which Spinoza aspired, and finally arrived at the fading Comprehension or Sensitivity Soul. But he was able to inject into his comprehensive view of nature an unlimited amount of that latter soul into the Consciousness Soul.

Michael earnestly observed this quest for man. But what he meant did enter into human spiritual development: *the* human being who once saw the essential intelligence when Michael still administered it from the cosmos. However, if it were not grasped with the spiritualized force of the Consciousness Soul, it would have to be extinguished and fall into the clutches of Lucifer's power. Michael's other great fear was that Lucifer could gain the upper hand if cosmic spirituality lost its equilibrium.

Michael's preparation for his mission at the end of the nineteenth century was in danger of becoming a cosmic tragedy. On earth great satisfaction reigned because of what had been learned about nature. But in Michael's domain a sense of tragedy existed because of the barriers to the introduction of the contrary image.

Previously Michael's austere, spiritualized love lived in the sun's rays, in the shimmering dawn and in the twinkling stars; now this love took on a note of deep sorrow when he observed humanity. Michael's situation in the cosmos became a difficult and tragic one, but also one which required an urgent solution at the moment when his earthly mission was imminent. Intellectuality could only be applied by humans to the body and its senses. They therefore had no insight into what their senses didn't tell them; their field of sense revelation was nature, but only thought of as matter. On the one hand they no longer witnessed divine spirituality in natural forms, but rather something spiritless, which was nevertheless presumed to bring forth the spirit in which man lives. On the other hand, they only wanted to accept from the spiritual world what was revealed in historical accounts. Spiritual observation of the past was just as scorned then as it is now.

Only what pertained to the present, where Michael did not enter, still lived in human souls. People were glad to stand on "solid" ground. They believed this because they did not have to look for what they feared were fantastic assumptions about nature. But Michael was not happy; he had to fight against Lucifer and Ahriman in his own domain. That resulted in great tragic difficulty because Lucifer could approach people that much easier to the extent that Michael, who was also protecting the past, had to keep his distance from them. Thus a mighty battle for humanity took place in the spiritual world immediately bordering the earth between Michael and Lucifer and Ahriman, while on earth man acted contrary to what was beneficial for the development of his soul. Of course all this is applicable to European and American spiritual life. For Asia one would have to speak differently.

Goetheanum, December 14, 1924

Further Guidelines, relating to the previous Third Contemplation

134. At the very beginning of the Conscious Soul times, man felt that the previous imaginative image of the human being, his own essence, had been lost. Incapable of finding it in the Consciousness Soul, he sought it in natural science or history. He wanted the old image of man to arise in him once again.

135. He did not, however, arrive at a true feeling for the human being, but rather to illusions. But he did not realize this and saw in them something substantial.

136. Therefore, during the time previous to his earthly activity, Michael observed human evolution with sorrow and pain. For man scorned all spiritual contemplation and therewith cut himself off from what bound him to Michael.

ANTHROPOSOPHICAL GUIDELINES

102

Christmas Contemplation: The Logos Mystery

The Mystery of Golgotha streams into the contemplation of the Michael-Mystery because of the fact that Michael is the force which leads man to Christ in a wholesome way.

But the Michael mission is one which repeats itself rhythmically in cosmic human evolution. It was repeatedly present in its beneficent effect on humanity before the Mystery of Golgotha. It was related to all the revelations that the still supra-earthly Christ forces were doing for man's evolution. After the Mystery of Golgotha it became subservient to the development of earthly humanity through Christ. It entered into a variegated and progressive form in its repetitions — but just that: repetitions.

In contrast, the Mystery of Golgotha is an all-embracing cosmic event which occurred only *once* during the course of cosmic human evolution.

As humanity advanced as far as the development of its Comprehension or Sensitivity Soul, the ever-present, potentially primeval danger of the separation of humanity from divine spirituality fully exerted itself. And in the same degree in which the human soul lost its experiencing of the divine-spiritual beings, it became immersed in what is today called "nature".

Man no longer saw the essence of humanity in the divine-spiritual cosmos; he saw the works of divine spirituality in the earthly domain. At first he did not see it in the abstract form in which it is seen today — as physical-sense being and events, which are condensed into the abstract ideas called "natural law". He saw it as a divine-spiritual nature. This divine-spiritual nature billowed in everything he saw in the emerging and dying out of animals, in the growth and sprouting of the plant world, in the flow of springs and rivers and in the formation of wind and clouds. He considered all this to be the gestures, deeds and speech of the godly being which is the foundation of "nature".

Just as the positions and movements of the stars were once seen by man to be the deeds and gestures of the universal divinity whose words could be read in them, now the "facts of nature" were seen to be an expression of the earth goddess — for the active goddess in nature was considered to be feminine. Vestiges of this way of thinking as imaginative content of the Comprehension or Sensitivity Soul were active in the human soul well into the middle ages.

Knowledgeable people spoke of the deeds of the "goddess" when they wanted to conceptualize "natural events". Only with the gradual emergence of the Consciousness Soul did this living, soul-filled consideration of nature become incomprehensible.

And the way in which this was seen in the Comprehension or Sensitivity Soul epoch is reminiscent of the Persephone myth with the mystery that is at its foundation. Demeter's daughter, Persephone, is forced by the god of the underworld to follow him into his kingdom. It turns out that she must spend only half of the time in the underworld, and the other half in the over-world. This myth expresses with great force how once in the remote past the evolution of the world was revealed through dreamlike clairvoyance.

In primeval times creative activity originated in the earth's surroundings. The earth itself was still in the process of becoming. It formed its being in cosmic evolution from the activities of its surroundings. The divine-spiritual beings of the cosmos crafted its being. When the earth was sufficiently developed to be an independent cosmic body, divine-spirituality came down to it from the cosmos and became earthly divinity. The dreamlike clairvoyance of humanity of that time knew and saw this fact; the Persephone myth is what remains of that knowledge. But what also remained was how humanity sought knowledge of "nature" until well into the middle ages. For one did not yet seek it by means of sense impressions, as was later the case — that is, according to what appears on the earth's surface, but according to the forces that work up from the depths of the earth. And these "forces of the depths", the "forces of the underworld", were observed in conjunction with the effects of the stars and elements of the earth's surroundings.

The plants grew there in a diversity of forms, and revealed themselves in their many-colored variety. The sun, moon and star forces worked in them together with the forces of the earth's depths.

Minerals, which were penetrated by what had become earthly from cosmic being, provided the basis for this. Rocks sprang up from the "underworld" only through the heavenly forces which had become earthly. The animal world had not absorbed the underworld forces. It arose only through the active cosmic forces in the earth's surroundings. It thanks the sun forces steaming down to the earth for its becoming, capacity for nourishment and movement. It reproduces under the influence of the moon forces streaming to the earth. It appears in many forms and species because the constellations act in the most varied way from the universe in shaping animal life. But the animals are only put down on the earth from the universe. With their dim consciousness they only participate in earthly matters; with their genesis, their growth, in fact with everything they are which allows them to perceive and move — they are not earthly beings.

This sublime concept of the earth's evolution once lived in humanity. What intruded in the Middle Ages left only a vestige of this concept as recognizable. It order to achieve knowledge of all this, one must be able to view the remote past with visionary knowledge. Because even using the existent physical documentation, only *he* can perceive what existed in human souls who can do so with spiritual vision.

Humanity is not able to hold the earth at arm's length to the extent the animals do. In saying this, one approaches the mystery of humanity as well as that of the animal world. These mysteries were reflected in the animal cults of ancient peoples, especially those of the Egyptians. They saw in the animals beings which are guests on the earth, in which one could visualize the beings and activities of the spiritual world that surrounds the earth. And in the connection of the human form with the animal form, which was portrayed in pictures, they visualized the form of those elementary intermediate beings who, although in the evolutionary process of becoming human, did not enter the earth's domain in order *not* to become human. Such elementary intermediate beings do exist. The Egyptians were only showing what they saw when they created images of them. But such beings do not have the full self-consciousness of humanity. In order to achieve that, the human being had to stride the earth so completely that he absorbed something of the earth-essence into his own essence.

He had to be exposed to the fact that in this earthly world the divine spirituality to which he was bound was present — *but only in its effects*. And just *because* only these effects, torn loose from their source, were present, the Luciferic and Ahrimanic beings gained access. Therefore it was necessary for man to make way for Lucifer's and Ahriman's forcibly interjected activities in a part of his evolution — the earthly part. This was possible without man being separated from what remained of his connection to divine spirituality as long as he had not yet advanced to the development of his Comprehension or Sensitivity Soul. What occurred then was a corruption of his physical, etheric and astral bodies. An older science knew this as something vital for the human being. It knew that it was necessary in order that consciousness advance to self-consciousness in man. In the teaching carried out in the places founded by Alexander the Great an Aristotelianism existed which, rightly understood, contained an essential element of this corruption in its psychology. It was only later that such ideas no longer contained this element.

In the time before the development of the Comprehension or Sensitivity Soul, the force of his divine-spiritual origin was still so interwoven in man that these forces streaming to the earth from their cosmic home could hold the intervening Luciferic and Ahrimanic powers in check — in equilibrium. From the human side, it was sufficient help to maintain this equilibrium when in the cultic and mystery rituals the *image* was created of the divine-spiritual being descending into Lucifer's and Ahriman's realm and then emerging victorious. One sees in the pictorial representations of the various people's rituals in the times previous to the Mystery of Golgotha what later became reality in the Mystery of Golgotha.

Once the Comprehension or Sensitivity Soul had developed, man could only be kept from being cut off from his divine-spiritual essence through reality. The divinity had to enter as an earthly Being into the earthly organization of the Comprehension or Sensitivity Soul. This was accomplished when the divine-spiritual Logos, Christ, bound his cosmic destiny with the earth for the benefit of humanity.

Persephone immersed herself into the earth in order to free the plant-world from having to form itself from what is merely earthly. This was the descent of a divine-spiritual being into nature. Persephone also experiences a kind of "resurrection" — but annually, in rhythmic sequence. This cosmos-to-earth event is in contrast to the descent of the Logos for the benefit of humanity. Persephone descended to order nature in its original orientation. Rhythm must underlie this; for the process of nature occurs rhythmically. The Logos descended into humanity. It happened once during human evolution. For *this* evolution is only *one* link in a gigantic cosmic rhythm in which humanity before becoming humanity was something quite different and after which will again be something quite different, whereas plant life, *as such*, repeats itself in short rhythms.

Man needs to view the Mystery of Golgotha in this light during the Consciousness Soul age. For during the Comprehension or Sensitivity Soul age the severance of humanity [from divine-spirituality] would have been a danger had the Mystery of Golgotha not occurred. In the Consciousness Soul age a complete darkening of the spiritual world in man's consciousness would have had to occur if the Consciousness Soul did not sufficiently strengthen itself for man to be able to look back with insight at his divine-spiritual origin. If he can though, he finds the cosmic Logos as the being which can lead him back. He pervades himself with the powerful image which reveals what happened on Golgotha.

And the beginning of this understanding is the love-filled grasping of the Cosmic-Consecration-Night [Christmas Eve], which is festively commemorated every year. For the strengthening of the Consciousness Soul — which initially receives intellectuality — takes place when it allows warm love to enter into that coldest soul-element. This warm love is most enhanced when it is applied to the child Jesus, who appears on earth on the Cosmic-Consecration-Night. Therewith man lets the highest earthly spiritual event, which was at the same time a physical one, work on his soul; he has started on the path of taking Christ into himself.

Nature must be recognized as the foundation of man's being which revealed itself as Persephone — or the being who was perceived when "nature" was spoken of during the Middle Ages — as the divine-spiritual origin and eternal force from which it, nature, was born and is continuously reborn.

The human world must be recognized in a way that it reveals in Christ the eternal Logos, which works with man's originally bonded divine-spiritual essence for the unfolding of his Spirit-Being.

To guide the human heart in love to this grand cosmic contiguity is the true meaning of this festive commemoration every year at the Cosmic Christmas Eve. If *such* love lives in human hearts, then it permeates the cold light element of the Consciousness Soul with fiery warmth. If this were to happen without the permeation of fiery warmth, then man would never achieve thorough spiritual fulfillment. He would perish in the coldness of intellectual consciousness, or he would have to exist in a spiritual life which doesn't advance to the Consciousness Soul. He would then stay behind in the unfolding of the Comprehension or Sensitivity Soul.

But the essence of the Consciousness Soul is not cold. It only seems to be so *at the beginning* of its unfolding, for it can only reveal its light-filled content at first, and not yet the cosmic warmth from which it precedes.

To feel and experience Christmas in this way can make the following real in the soul: *how the glory of the divine-spiritual beings' revelations are announced to man in the vastness of the stars through their images, and how the liberation of humanity on earth from the powers that want to distance it from its origins is achieved.*

Goetheanum, on Christmas 1924

Additional Guidelines relating to the foregoing Christmas Contemplation

137. The activity in human and world evolution, which occurs due to Michael forces, *repeats itself rhythmically*, although in varying and progressing forms, before and after the Mystery of Golgotha.

138. The Mystery of Golgotha is the greatest *single* event in human evolution. It has nothing to do with rhythmic repetition. For although human evolution is part of a vast cosmic rhythm, it is nevertheless only *one* element — albeit the most extensive element in this rhythm. Before humanity became an element of this rhythm it was something substantially different; afterwards it will again be something different. Therefore during human evolution there are many Michael-events, but only one Golgotha event.

139. In the rapid rhythmic repetitions of a year, the divine-spiritual Being who descended to the depths of the earth accomplishes the task of spiritually permeating the processes of nature. She personifies the ensouling of nature with the original and eternal *forces* which must remain active, just as the descended Christ represents the ensouling of humanity with the original and eternal *Logos* who shall never cease his activities for the healing of humanity.

Heavenly History — Mythological History; Earthly History — The Mystery of Golgotha

In the spatial cosmos the universe and the earth's center stand in opposition. In the universe the stars are, in a sense, "disseminated". From the earth's center forces stream out to all directions of the universe.

In the contemporary cosmic epoch, the brilliance of the stars and the earth's forces can only appear to man as the works of the divine-spiritual Beings with whom he is inwardly united.

But a cosmic epoch once existed when the brilliance of the stars and the earth's forces were still the direct spiritual revelation of the divine-spiritual Beings. In his dim consciousness man felt the divine-spiritual Beings as being active in *his* being.

Another epoch ensued. The starry heaven, as a physical entity, separated itself from divine-spiritual activity. What one may call world-spirit and world-body arose. The world-spirit is a multiplicity of divine-spiritual Beings. During the older epoch they worked from the stars' positions down to the earth. What shone down from the vastness of the universe; what streamed as forces from the earth's center, were in reality the divine-spiritual Beings' intelligence and will working on the earth and its humanity.

During the later cosmic epochs — after the [ancient] Saturn and Sun evolutions — the divine-spiritual Beings' intelligence and will remained ever more spiritually contained within them. Where they were originally actively present became "world-body" — the harmonious configuration of the stars in space. Looking back on these things from a spiritually appropriate worldview, one can say: from the original spirit-body of the world's creative Beings, the world-spirit and the world-body arose. And the world-body shows in the configuration and movement of the stars how the intelligence and will of the gods *once* worked. But at the present cosmic time what was once freely moving divine intelligence and will in the stars has become fixed and subject to laws.

Therefore what today shines down to humanity on earth from the stars is not a direct expression of divine will and intelligence, but an inert symbol of what it once was *in the stars*. So in the human soul's admiration for the formations of heaven's stars one sees a past, but not a contemporary revelation of the gods. But what is "in the past" in the stars' shining is "contemporary" in the Spirit-World. And Man lives in this "contemporary" World-Spirit.

In respect to the formation of the world, one must look back to an *old* cosmic epoch in which World-Spirit and World-Body acted as a unity. One must then look at the *middle* epoch, during which they evolved into a duality. And one must think into the future, the *third* epoch, in which the World-Spirit will again enfold the World-Body in its actions. For the *old* epoch, the constellations and the paths of the stars were not to be *calculated,* for they were the expression of the free intelligence and the free will of divine-spiritual beings. In the future they will again be incalculable.

"Calculation" is only meaningful for the middle cosmic epoch. And as it is for the constellations and the paths of the stars, this also applies to the forces streaming from the earth's center into space. What comes "from the depths" will be "calculable". But everything strove from the older cosmic epochs towards the *middle* ones, in which space and time became "calculable" and divine-spirituality, as the revelation of intelligence and will, had to be sought "behind" the calculable.

Only during this middle epoch were the conditions present in which humanity could advance from a dim consciousness to a clear, free self-awareness and to a free intelligence and will.

A time had to come in which Copernicus and Kepler "calculated" the World-Body. For it was through the cosmic forces which accompanied this moment that human self-awareness had to develop. In the older age, this self-awareness was predisposed; then came a time of such advancement that the universe was "calculated".

On the earth "history" was acted out. It would never have happened had the universe's constellations and paths of stars not become "fixed". In the history of earth's evolution there exists a mirror image — but a completely transformed one — of what was once "heavenly history". More ancient peoples are still conscious of this "heavenly history", and they look to it far more than to "earthly history". In "earthly history" man's intelligence and will at first lived in association with the gods' cosmic divine will and intelligence, then independently.

In "heavenly history" live the intelligence and will of the divine-spiritual Beings directly related to humanity.

Looking back at the spiritual life of peoples in the far-distant past, a consciousness of togetherness and desire for togetherness with the divine-spiritual Beings existed within humanity, to the extent that their history was heavenly history. When they told of their "origins", they didn't mean earthly events, but cosmic ones. Even in relation to their own time, it seemed to them that what was happening in the earthly environment was unimportant compared to the cosmic events; and it was these latter to which their attention was directed.

An epoch existed in which man's consciousness viewed heavenly history in powerful impressions in which the divine-spiritual Beings themselves stood before him. They spoke; and the people heard the speech in dream-inspiration; they revealed their forms; and the people viewed them in dream-imagination.

This "heavenly history", which filled human souls for a long time, was followed by mythical history, which is often taken today to have been poetic versions. They conjoined heavenly history with earthly history. For example "heroes" appeared, superhuman beings. They were beings who stood higher in evolution than man who, at a certain time, had only developed up to his Sentient-Soul. The "hero" however, had already developed what in man will one day be the Spirit-Self. The "hero" could not directly incorporate within earthly conditions; he could, however, do so by immersing himself in a human soul and thus be capable of acting as a human among humans. These were the "initiates" of ancient times.

The people in the continuing epochs did not actually think of them in this way; rather, the things which occurred between the more spiritually incalculable and the physically calculable world underwent changes. What is certain, however, is that long after conditions had changed, the consciousness of one people or another held fast to a "worldview" which corresponded to a much earlier reality. At first this happened in a way that human consciousness which had not kept up with cosmic events really saw the past. Then came a time when the ability to see faded away and the past was only retained through tradition. Thus during the middle ages an interjection of the heavenly world into the earthly one was still traditionally retained, but no longer seen because the force behind the capacity to see in pictures no longer existed.

And on earth the various peoples evolved in such a way that they held fast to one or another worldview, so that different worldviews existed *alongside* each other, which in essence were successive ones. But the difference in worldviews was not only due to this, but also because the different peoples, according to their natures, saw different things. The Egyptians saw the world in which there were Beings who prematurely ended their evolution and never became human beings; and they also saw man after his life on earth in all that associated him with those beings. The Chaldean people saw more how outer-earthly spiritual beings — good and evil — entered earthly life in order to be active there.

The very long duration of "heavenly history" was followed by "mythological" history, which was shorter, but compared to later actual "history", nevertheless lasted for a long time indeed.

As I have already explained, in his consciousness man abandoned with difficulty the old visions in which gods and men were conceived of as acting together. Thus "actual earth science" has existed since the unfolding of the Comprehension or Sensitivity Soul. Man "thought" in the sense of what previously existed. Only when the first germs of the Consciousness Soul evolved did man begin to conceive of "history proper".

And in what has been detached from divine-spirituality and become human-spiritual history, can be experienced by man as free intelligence and free will. Thus the development of the world in which man is engrossed runs its course between the fully calculable and the activity of free intelligence and free will. The evolution of the world manifests itself in all the intermediate nuances of both.

Man lives his life between birth and death in a way that unfolds in the calculable the physical foundation for the creation of his inner divine-spiritual free incalculability. His life between death and a new birth runs its course in the incalculable — in a way, however, that in the "interior" of his divine-spiritual being the calculable unfolds in thought. By means of this calculability he becomes the architect of his future earthly life. In "history" the calculable exists on earth, in which, however, the incalculable is contained, if only to limited degree.

The Luciferic and Ahrimanic beings oppose the order between the incalculable and the calculable established from the beginning by the divine-spiritual beings united with humanity; they oppose their harmonization through "measurement, number and weight". Lucifer, by his very nature, cannot integrate anything which is calculable. His ideal is unconditional intelligence and will.

This Luciferic tendency is appropriate to the cosmic order in areas in which free acts should reign. There Lucifer is the justified spiritual helper in human development. Without his help freedom in human divine-spirituality, which is built on the foundation of physical calculability, could not enter. But Lucifer would like to extend this tendency to the entire cosmos. And here his activity comes into conflict with the divine-spiritual order, to which man originally belongs.

This is where Michael enters. He stands with his own being in the incalculable; but he effectuates a balance between the incalculable and the calculable, which he bears within him as the Cosmic Thought that he received from his gods.

The Ahrimanic powers in the world are different. They are the complete opposite of the divine-spiritual Beings with whom man has been bound from the beginning. These divine-spiritual Beings are presently purely spiritual powers, who possess perfectly free intelligence and perfectly free will, but who within this free intelligence and free will conceive the wise insight of the necessity for the calculable, the unfree, as Cosmic Thought — from whose womb man is to develop into a free being. And they are united to all that is calculable, to Cosmic Thought, *with love*. This loves streams out from them through the universe.

The greedy lust and *cold hate* of the Ahrimanic powers for everything that promotes freedom is the antithesis of this. Ahriman strives to make everything that he streams out from the earth into universal space a cosmic machine. His ideal is exclusively "measurement, number and weight". He was called into the cosmos which serves human evolution because it was necessary for "measurement, number and weight", his field, to unfold.

Only he who understands the world spiritually and physically in *all its aspects*, truly understands it. This understanding must reach into nature in respect to such powers as the divine-spiritual ones who work with love, and the Ahrimanic ones who work with hate. One must perceive the divine-spiritual Beings' love active in nature's cosmic warmth that begins in springtime and increases towards summer; one must be aware of Ahriman's activity in winter's gusting frost.

The appearance every year of this divine love is the time of remembrance, for the free element of God entered into the calculable element of earth with Christ. Christ acts in complete freedom in the calculable; he thereby renders harmless what lusts only for the calculable, the Ahrimanic.

The event of Golgotha is the free cosmic deed of love in earthly history; it is only comprehensible by the love which humanity brings to this comprehension.

Goetheanum, Christmas, 1924

140. Cosmic events, in which human evolution is interlinked, and which in human consciousness reflects "history" in a broad sense, is subdivided in the long-lasting heavenly history, the shorter mythological history and in the relatively short earthly history.

141. Presently these cosmic events are segregated into the "incalculable" activity of divine-spiritual beings, who create

with free intelligence and will, and the "calculable" occurrence of the world-body.

142. The Luciferic powers stand opposed to the calculability of the world-body; the Ahrimanic powers stand opposed to the creation of free intelligence and free will.

143. The event of Golgotha is a free cosmic deed which descends from Universal Love and can only be grasped through human love.

What is Revealed when One Looks Back at Repeated Earth Lives

When spiritual cognition can look back at a person's previous earth lives, what is revealed is that a number of such earth lives existed in which the human being was already an individual. Outwardly he was similar to today, and he had an inner life which contained individual characteristics. Earth lives appear which indicate when the Comprehension or Sensitivity Soul existed but not yet the Consciousness Soul, and other lives when only the Sentient Soul had evolved, and so forth. In the earth's historical ages this is the case, and it was the case for a long time previously as well.

But one also perceives ages when this was not yet the case. There one finds man still interlinked in his inner life and outer formation with the world of divine-spiritual Beings. Man existed as earthly humanity, but was not yet separated from divine-spiritual being, thinking and willing.

In still older times man completely disappears as a separate entity; only divine-spiritual Beings exist, who bear humanity in their fold.

Man has passed through these three stages of his evolution during his time on earth. The transition from the first to the second stage took place towards the end of Lemuria, from the second to the third during the age of Atlantis.

Just as man carries his experiences as remembrance within him in his current earthly life, he also carries within him as cosmic memory everything that he experienced as described above. What is earthly soul-life? The world of remembrances, which is prepared at every moment to perceive anew. Man lives out his inner earthly existence in this interaction of remembering and new experiences.

But this inner earthly existence could not unfold if cosmic remembrance did not still now exist in man when he looks back spiritually to the first stage of his becoming an earthly being, in which he had not yet been separated from divine-spiritual being.

From what happened at that time, only what develops within the human nervous-sensory organization still exists. In outer nature all

119

the forces which were then active have died out and are only perceptible as dead forms.

Thus what exists in human thought as contemporary revelation is the necessary basis for earthly existence: what had already developed before he attained to an individual earthly existence.

In life between death and a new birth man experiences this stage ever anew. Only he also brings his individual existence, fully formed during his lives on earth, into the world of divine-spiritual Beings, which again takes him in, the same world which once included him in it. Between death and a new birth he is in the present, but at the same time he is in all the time which he has passed through in repeated earth lives and repeated lives between death and new births.

It is different in respect to his world of feeling. This world is related to the experiences which occurred directly after those which he had before he became completely human. These are the experiences he passed through as a human being, but when he had not yet separated from divine-spiritual being, thinking and willing. At present man could develop no world of feeling if it did not arise on the basis of his rhythmic organization — in which the cosmic memory of the above-mentioned second stage of human evolution exists. Thus in man's world of feeling his spiritual present works together with his experiences from an older time.

In the life between death and a new birth man experiences the content of the time here described as the outer boundary of his cosmos. What the stars in heaven are for man in his physical earth life, spiritually is his Being in the life between death and a new birth — which lies between his complete solidarity with the divine-spiritual world and his separation from it. There at the" boundary of the world" the physical heavenly bodies do not appear to him; rather on every star the sum of the divine-spiritual Beings, who are, in reality, the star.

With the will alone, not associated with feeling and thinking, man lives in what his observed earth lives reveal to be personal and individual. What comes from the outer cosmos as his outer form is preserved as cosmic remembrance; it lives in the human form as forces. They are not directly the will's forces, but what constitutes the foundation of the will's forces in the human organization. In life between death and a new birth *this* area lies outside the "boundary of the world". Man thinks of it there as something he will regain in his new earth life.

In his nervous-sensible-organization man is today still united with the cosmos as he was when he was still germinally developing within divine-spirituality.

In his rhythmical organization man still lives today in the cosmos as he did when, although already existing as human, he was not yet separated from divine-spirituality.

In his metabolism-limbs organization — the basis for the development of his will — everything he passed through since the beginning of his personal, individual earth lives and the lives between death and new births produce after-effects in this organization.

From the forces of the earth man only has what bestows self-consciousness. The physical-corporal foundation for this self-consciousness also derives from the earth's activity. Everything else in the human being is of outer-earthly, cosmic origin. The feeling and thinking astral body and its etheric-physical foundation, all the active life elements in the etheric body, even the chemically reacting elements in his physical body have an outer-earthly origin. Strange as it may be sound, the active physical-chemical elements in the human being do not derive from the earth.

That man develops these outer-earthy cosmic elements within him is due to the activity of the *planets* and the other *stars.* The *sun,* through its forces, brings all these developments to the earth. The human-cosmic is transferred by the sun to the earthly domain. Through the sun man lives on the earth as a heavenly being. Only what transcends his own development, namely the capacity to reproduce, is a gift of the moon.

Of course these are not the only effects of the sun and moon. Other highly spiritual activities also originate in them.

When at Christmas time the sun acquires ever more forces for the earth, it constitutes the rhythmically manifesting yearly activity in the physical earth, which is an expression of the spirit in nature.

Human evolution is a single element in a virtually gigantic cosmic year. This is evident from the preceding explanations. In this cosmic year, the Cosmic Christmas is where the sun not merely affects the earth through the spirit of nature, but where the sun's soul, the Christ-Spirit, descends to the earth.

As in the individual, what is personally experienced is associated with cosmic remembrance, Christmas is correctly felt by the human soul every year if the heavenly-cosmic Christ event is thought of as *continuous* — and as not merely human, but as cosmic remembrance. Not only man, but also the cosmos celebrates the descent of Christ at Christmas.

Goetheanum, New Year, 1925

144. When one looks back at the repeated earth lives of a person, they arrange themselves in three different stages: the oldest, in which man was not yet an individual, but existed germinally in divine-spirituality. One does not find a human being when looking back, but divine-spiritual Beings (The Ur-Forces, Archai).

145. Then comes an intermediate stage in which man already exists as an individual being, but is not yet separated from the Thinking, Willing and Being of the divine-spiritual world. He did not yet have his present personality, was not yet completely his own being in his existence on earth, and was not yet separated from the divine-spiritual world.

146. The third stage emerges as the present. Man experiences himself in his human form as detached from the divine-spiritual world; and he experiences the world as the environment which he confronts personally and individually. This stage began during the age of Atlantis.

What is Revealed when between Death and a New Birth, One Looks Back into Previous Lives — Part 1

In the previous contemplation human life in its entirety was followed with emphasis on successive earth lives. The other viewpoint, which can shed more light on what the previous one reveals, is the contemplation of successive lives between death and a new birth. It also shows that the substance of these lives (as they are now) only goes back to a certain point of time in the earth's evolution. *This* substance is determined by the fact that one carries through the portal of death the inner force of self-consciousness acquired during his earth life. It enables him to stand as a complete individuality amidst the divine-spiritual Beings.

During a preceding period this was not the case. At that time man was still not very advanced in the development of his self-consciousness. The forces acquired on earth were not sufficient to disconnect him from the divine-spiritual world and to have an individual existence between death and a new birth. This doesn't mean that man found himself in the divine-spiritual Beings, rather within their sphere of activity, to the extent that his will was essentially *their* will, and not his own.

Before that period, another existed in which when looking back at it one does not find man as he is in his contemporary soul-constitution, but in the world of divine-spiritual Beings, in which man existed in a germinal stage. Those Beings are the Primal Forces, (Archai).

Therefore when tracing back the life path of *one* individual, not *one* divine-spiritual Being is encountered, but all who belong to that hierarchy. The will that man shall come into being lives in these divine-spiritual Beings. All of them participate in the will that each human individual shall come into being. The cosmic objective of their choirlike cooperation is the genesis of the human *form*. For man still lived without form in the divine-spiritual world.

It may seem odd that the whole choir of divine-spiritual Beings should work for *one* human being. However, even earlier the Exusiai, Dynameis, Kyriotetes, Throne, Cherubim and Seraphim hierarchies worked in this way during the [ancient] Moon, Sun and Saturn stages in order than man could come into being.

What originated earlier on Saturn, Sun and Moon, a kind of pre-human, did not possess a unified form. Pre-humans existed who were organized more according to the limbs system, others more according to the breast system, again others who were organized according to the head system. They were really human beings; they are described here as pre-humans in order to differentiate them from the later stages when the balanced confluence of all the systems appeared in the human form. The differentiation of those pre-humans goes much further. One can speak of heart-people, lung-people, and so on.

The Primal Forces hierarchy considered that its mission was to integrate those pre-humans — whose soul-lives still corresponded to their one-sided forms — into the general human form. They took over humanity from the hands of the Exusiai, who had already *in thought* created a unity from human multiplicity. However, for the Exusiai this unity was still an ideal form, a cosmic thought form. The Archai shaped the etheric form, but in such a way that it contained the forces for the development of the physical form.

Observation of these occurrences reveals something wonderful — that the human being is the ideal and the objective of the gods. But this observation cannot be the source of vanity and pride. For each can only take credit for what he has made of himself in his earth life with self-consciousness. And this, expressed cosmically, is little compared to what the gods have achieved from the macrocosm — which *they* are — as the basis for his selfhood as microcosm — which *he* is.

The divine-spiritual Beings face each other in the cosmos. The visible expression of this stance is the shape of the star-filled sky. They wanted to create as a unity in humanity what they are all together.

In order to correctly understand what the hierarchy of the Archai accomplished in their choir when they created the human form one must realize that there is a great difference between this form and the human physical body. The physical body is composed of physical-chemical processes. These take place in contemporary man within his human form. But the form itself is spiritual through and through. To perceive with our physical senses in the physical world something spiritual as the human form should be a solemn experience. For someone who can see spiritually, this means seeing in the human form a true imagination that has descended to the physical world. If one wishes to see imaginations, he must pass over from the physical word to the next-lying spiritual one. Then he will realize how the human form is related to these imaginations.

When observing life between death and a new birth, human spiritual vision finds the genesis of the human form as the first period. At the same time the deep relationship between man and the hierarchy of the Archai is revealed. In this period one can have an *inkling* of the difference between earth life and life between death and a new birth. Namely the hierarchy of the Archai works creating the human form in rhythmical epochs. During one period it directs the thoughts which guide the individual wills more towards the outer-earthy cosmos. During another one it looks down upon the earth. And from the concurrence of what comes from the outer-earthly cosmos and what is stimulated from the earth, the human form is structured, which constitutes the expression of the fact that man is simultaneously an earthly and an outer-earthly cosmic being.

The human form, described here as the creation of the hierarchy of the Archai, embraces not merely man's the external outline and the surface formation as determined by the skin, but also the formation of forces in his posture, in his capacity for movement corresponding to earthly conditions and in the capacity to use his body as the expression of his inner self.

That man can insert himself with upright posture in the earth's gravity, that he can freely move with equilibrium in this gravity, that he can wrest his arms and hands from gravity and use them freely — this and much more that is surely within him but is nevertheless formative: all this man owes to the creative acts of the hierarchy of the Archai. All this was prepared in the life between death and a new birth, which one can also call this period. Preparations were made so that in the third period, in our present time, man himself has the capacity during his life between death and a new birth to work on this formation for his earthly existence.

Goetheanum, at the New Year, 1925

147. Life between death and a new birth also indicates three periods. In the first man lives entirely in the hierarchy of the Archai. His future human form for [use in] the physical world is prepared by them.

148. The Archai prepare the human being in order that he can later develop his free self-consciousness; for this [self-consciousness] can only be developed in beings who, through the form thus created, and from an inner impulse of the soul, embody it.

149. This shows how the kernel of human attributes and forces which manifest themselves in our time were predisposed during ages long past, and how the microcosm grows out of the macrocosm.

What is Revealed when between Death and a New Birth, One Looks Back into Previous Lives — Part 2

In a second period man passed out of the Archai realm into that of the Archangeloi, with whom he was not as bodily-spiritually bonded as previously with the Archai. His bonding with the Archangels was more spiritual. But it was still intimate enough that one cannot yet speak of a separation from the divine-spiritual world.

The Archangel hierarchy gave to man's etheric body the element which corresponds to what the Archai gave to his physical body. Just as the physical body's form is adapted to the earth in order to become the vehicle of self-consciousness, the etheric body is adapted to the outer-earthly cosmic forces. The earth lives in the physical body and the star-world lives in the etheric body. The inner force that enables the human being to live on the earth and at the same time wrest himself from it through posture, movement and gesture, he owes to the Archangels' creative activity in his etheric body. Just as the earth-forces can exist in the physical body through the figuration, so do the forces exist in the etheric body that stream to the earth from all sides of the circumference of the cosmos. The living earth forces which appear physically in the body are those that make its form relatively firm and enclosed. The human contours remain fixed for earthly life subject to a subordinate metamorphosis; the capacity for movement solidifies through habit, etc.

In the etheric body there is permanent flexible mobility, which is a mirror image of the ever changing constellations during a person's life on earth. Even the changing sky by day and night corresponds to the shaping of the etheric body — but also the changes that take place during the time between birth and death

This adaptation of the etheric body to the heavenly forces does not contradict the gradual separation of the stars in the sky from the divine-spiritual powers as described in the previous contemplation. It is correct that in very old times divine will and divine intelligence lived in the stars. In later times the stars became "calculable". The gods were no longer active in their creation. But through his etheric body man gradually attained his own relationship to the stars, as he did to the earth's gravity through his physical body.

The etheric body, created during the second period by the Archangeloi hierarchy and inserted in man when he descends from the spiritual world to earth at birth, absorbs the extra-earthly cosmic forces.

An essential aspect which man received through this hierarchy is that of belonging to a group of people on earth. People are differentiated all over the earth. When looking back at this second period, one does not see the present day differentiation of races and peoples, but a somewhat different, more spiritual one. This is attributable to the star forces in the different constellations appearing at different locations on earth. On the earth in the distribution of land and water, in the climate, in plant growth and so on, live the stars. Insofar man must adapt to *these* conditions on earth, which are conditions of the heavens, this adaptation belongs to the etheric body and is a creation of the Archangeloi choir.

However, it was just during this second period that the Luciferic and Ahrimanic powers entered into human life in a special way. This was necessary, although at first it seems that man was being driven to a *lower* level of his nature. If man was to develop self-consciousness in his earthly life, it was necessary that he separate himself from the divine-spiritual world from which he originated to a greater extent that was possible by means of *that* world itself. It happened during the time when the Archangels acted upon him, for then the spiritual force of the Archangels was less able to keep Lucifer and Ahriman at bay then when the stronger Archai forces acted upon him.

The Luciferic powers caused a stronger inclination in the etheric body towards the stars than it would have had if only the divine-spiritual powers originally bound to man had been active. And the physical organization was made more subject to the earth's gravity than would have happened had these powers been unable to act.

In this way the seed of complete self-consciousness and free will was planted in man. Even though the ahrimanic powers hate free will, they brought about the predisposition for free will *in man* by detaching him from *his* divine-spiritual world.

First, however, in that second period what the various hierarchies, from the Seraphim to the Archangels, brought about in man was impressed more into the physical and etheric bodies than would have happened without the luciferic and ahrimanic influences. Without these influences the activities of the hierarchies would have remained more in the astral body and the I. By this means the more spiritual groupings of humanity over the earth striven for by the Archangels did not occur.

Being impressed into the physical and etheric bodies, the spiritual forces were transformed into their opposite. A differentiation according to races and peoples instead of the more spiritual one took place.

Without the luciferic and ahrimanic influences the people on earth would see themselves as having been differentiated from heaven. The groups would have comported themselves in their lives as beings who willingly give to and take the spiritual from each other lovingly. In races and ethnic groups the earth's gravity appears through the human body; in the spiritual groupings a mirror image of the spiritual world would have appeared.

Because of all this, the later complete self-consciousness in human evolution had to be predisposed beforehand. This also required, although in a diminished form, that the primeval human differentiation which existed when man first passed from the hierarchy of the Exusiai to that of the Archai be preserved.

Man experienced — through feeling and envisioning — this stage of evolution in a kind of cosmic school, although he had not yet developed the knowledge that this was an essential preparation for his later self-consciousness. But the felt envisioning of his evolution forces was nevertheless important then for the integration of self-consciousness in his astral body and I.

In respect to thinking, what happened was that man was equipped by the luciferic powers with a tendency to immerse himself further in the old spiritual forms and not to adapt to the new forms. For Lucifer always strives to retain the previous forms of life for man.

And thereby man's thinking was organized in such a way that in life between death and a new birth he gradually developed the capacities which formed thoughts in him in primeval times. *At that time* these faculties could visualize the spiritual, despite being akin to present-day mere sense perception. For the physical bore the spiritual in its surface. At present however, the capacities for thought preserved from those times can only function as sense perception. Gradually the ability to elevate one's self to the spiritual world diminished. And this is fully the case now when in the Consciousness Soul age the spiritual world has become veiled in darkness for man. Thus in the nineteenth century the best natural scientists, who could not become materialists, said: we have no choice but to *merely* investigate the world that can be investigated with the senses through measurement, number and weight; but we have no right to deny a spiritual world which is hidden behind the senses. That is, an indication that a light-filled world, *unknown* to man, could exist where he only stares into the darkness.

As thinking was dislocated by Lucifer, willing was by Ahriman. Man's will was endowed with a tendency to a kind of freedom, which should have happened only later. This freedom was not *real*, but an *illusion* of freedom. Humanity lived for a long time with this illusion of freedom. It provided humanity with no possibility of spiritually developing the idea of freedom. It swung back and forth between the opinion that man is free or that he is trapped in a rigid necessity. And when true freedom arrived with the emerging Consciousness Soul age, man could not recognize it, because he had been trapped much too long in the illusion of freedom.

Everything that had been instilled in man in this second stage of evolution of his lives between death and a new birth he carried as cosmic remembrance into the third stage, the one in which he presently lives. During this stage he stands in a similar relationship to the hierarchy of the Angeloi as he did during the second stage to that of the Archangeloi. Only the relationship to the Angeloi is one in which full independent individuality is realized. For the Angeloi — now not the choir, but *one* for *each* person — concentrate on achieving the correct relation between the lives between death and a new birth and earth lives.

What at first appears to be a remarkable fact is that for the *individual* during the second stage of his evolution of lives between death and a new birth the entire hierarchy of archangeloi was active. Later this hierarchy assumed the guidance of ethnic groups, in which *one* archangel acted as ethnic spirit for a people. The Primal Forces [Archai] remained active in the races. And a Being from the hierarchy of the Primal Forces acted as race-spirit for *one* race.

Thus contemporary humanity retains — also in life between death and a new birth — the cosmic remembrance of previous stages of evolution. And also where in the physical world spiritual guidance appears, as in races and ethnic groups, this comic remembrance is distinctly present.

Goetheanum, New Year, 1925

150. In a second period of evolution of lives between death and a new birth, man entered the realm of the Archangeloi. During this period, after it had been predisposed in the creation of the human form during the first period, the seed was implanted in the soul for his later self-consciousness.

151. During this second period man was pushed deeper into the physical world due to the Luciferic and Ahrimanic influences than he would have been without these influences.

152. During the third period man entered the realm of the Angeloi, who however only made their influence felt in the astral body and the I. This period is the present one. What happened in the two previous periods lives on in human evolution and explains the fact that in the age of the Consciousness Soul (in the nineteenth century) man stared into the spiritual world as into complete darkness.

What is the Reality of the Earth within the Macrocosm?

In these contemplations we have viewed the evolution of the cosmos and of the earth from the most varied viewpoints. We have shown how the forces of man's being come from the outer-earthly cosmos, except for those which give him his self-consciousness. These come to him from the earth. This indicates the meaning of the earth for humanity. But it brings up another question: What is the meaning of the earth for the macrocosm?

In order to approach the answer to this question it is necessary to review what has already been said.

The seer's consciousness finds the macrocosm increasingly alive as it penetrates further into the past. In the distant past all calculability of its nature ceases. Man was separated from this nature. The macrocosm entered ever further into the sphere of the calculable. In the process, however, it gradually died. In the measure in which man — the microcosm — emerged from the macrocosm as an independent being, the former gradually died.

In the cosmic present a dead macrocosm exists. But in this evolutionary process not only man arose. The earth also arose from the macrocosm. Man, who derives the forces for his self-consciousness from the earth, is much too close to it to clearly understand its nature. In the full enfolding of self-consciousness during the Consciousness Soul age, man has become accustomed to direct his attention to the spatial magnitude of the universe and to consider the earth as being a kind of dust-particle, inconsequential when compared to the physical space of the universe.

It will therefore seem strange at first when spiritual observation reveals the true cosmic meaning of this so-called "dust-particle".

The vegetable and animal kingdoms are embedded in the earth's mineral foundation. In all of them live the forces which appear in their various forms during the seasons. Look at the plant world. In autumn and winter it displays dying forces. The seer's consciousness perceives in these forms the essence of the forces which have brought about the macrocosm's process of dying. In spring and summer the forces of growth and sprouting are evident in plant life.

The seer's consciousness does not only see in this growth and sprouting what is blessed by plant life during the year, but a *surplus* — a surplus of germinating forces. The plants receive more germination force than they expend for the growth of leaves, flowers and fruit. This surplus of germinating forces streams out into the outer-earthly cosmos before the seer's vision.

In the same way, surplus force from the mineral kingdom streams out into the outer-earthly cosmos. *This* force has the task of bringing the forces that come from the plants to the correct regions of the cosmos. Under the influence of the mineral forces a newly formed image of a cosmos is created by the plant forces.

There are also forces that come from the animals. These do not act as the mineral and plant forces do, streaming out from the earth, but they gather what the mineral and plant forces have carried to the universe and combine them into a sphere (globe) and create therewith the image of an enclosed macrocosm.

This is how the spiritually cognitional consciousness perceives the essence of the earthly domain. *It exists within the dead macrocosm giving new life.* Just as from a seed, which is so insignificantly small, a very large plant emerges when the old one dies and disintegrates, a new macrocosm will come into being from the "dust particle" earth when the old one disintegrates.

That is a true vision of the earth's essence, that in all its parts a universe is germinating. One obtains an understanding of the kingdoms of nature *only* by sensing this germinating element in it. Within this germinating life man undertakes his earthly existence. He participates in the germinating as well as in the dying processes. He derives his thinking forces from the dying element. As long as these thinking forces came in the past from the still living macrocosm, they were not the foundation of the self-conscious human being. The acted as growth forces in human beings who still had no self-consciousness. The thinking forces, *in themselves*, may not have a life of their own if they are to form the foundation for free human self-consciousness. Together with the dead macrocosm, they must, in themselves, be the dead *shadows* of the cosmic past.

On the other hand, man participates in the earth's germinating processes. His will forces come from them. They are life itself, but man does not participate in their essence with his self-consciousness. They radiate into the shadows of thought within the human being. The shadows of thought stream through them and in this streaming of free thought in the germinating earth full, free human self-consciousness enters humanity in the Consciousness Soul age.

The past casting shadows and the future containing the seeds of reality meet each other in the human being. And this meeting is human life in the present. That this is so is immediately evident to the seer's consciousness when it finds itself in the spirit-region which borders directly on the physical one, and in which one also finds Michael's field of activity.

All earthly life becomes transparent when one senses the seed of the universe in its foundation. Every plant form, every stone — they appear to the human soul in a new light when it realizes that every one of these things contributes by its life, by its form, to the earth being the embryonic seed of a new revivifying macrocosm. If one only tries to bring to life his thinking about these facts, he will realize what it can mean for humanity's sensibility.

Goetheanum, January 1925

153. During the beginning of the Consciousness Soul age, people had become accustomed to concentrate on the spatial-physical grandeur of the universe, and above all to be sensible only of *this*. Therefore one called the earth a "dust particle" within the physically immense universe.

154. This "dust particle" reveals itself to clairvoyant consciousness as the seed of a newly developing macrocosm, while the old one dies out. It had to die in order that man could separate himself from it in full self-consciousness.

155. In the cosmic present, man participates with his liberating thinking forces in what has died [the macrocosm], and with his will forces — concealed from him in their essence — in the earth's germinating, revivifying new macrocosm.

Sleeping and Waking in Light of the preceding Contemplations

Sleeping and Waking have often been considered within anthroposophical contemplations from various points of view. But understanding of such facts of life must always be intensified anew when other subjects concerning the world are considered. The contemplation that the earth is a seed for a newly emerging macrocosm presents an opportunity for enhanced understanding of the phenomena of sleeping and waking.

When awake, man lives in the thought-shadows which are emitted from a dying world — and in the impulses of will, the innermost essence of which he perceives as little with normal consciousness as he perceives what takes place during deep dreamless sleep. By the induction of these subconscious impulses of will into the thought-shadows, autonomous self-consciousness arises. The "I" lives in this self-consciousness.

As man experiences his surroundings in this state, his inner feelings are penetrated by outer-earthly cosmic impulses which enter the present from a far distant cosmic past. He is not conscious of this. A being can only be conscious of what he participates in with his own dying forces, and not with growing forces that give life to that being. Thus man is conscious of himself in that he loses sight of the foundation of his being. But it is just because of this that he is in a position to sense himself completely in the thought-shadows while in the waking state. No reviving element hinders his inner being from participating in the process of dying out. But this "living in the dying" conceals the nature of the earth as the seed of a new universe. In the waking state man does not perceive the earth as it is; its incipient cosmic life is concealed.

Man lives thus in what the earth gives him as the foundation of his self-consciousness. In the age of self-conscious I-enfolding, he loses spiritual sight of the true nature of his inner impulses as well as those of his surroundings. But it is just in this hovering over the world-being that he experiences the being of his I; he experiences himself as a self-conscious being. Above him the outer-earthly cosmos, below him the earth — a world whose true essence remains hidden; between them the revelation of the free "I", whose true essence radiates the full resplendence of knowledge and free will.

It is otherwise during sleep, when man's astral body and his I live in the seed nature of the earth. The most intensive "urge for new life" acts in human surroundings in dreamless sleep. And his dreams are permeated by this life, but not so strongly as to prevent him from experiencing them in a kind of semi-consciousness. In this semiconscious observation of dreams one sees the forces through which the human being is woven from the cosmos. In the flash of dreams the astral enlivening of man streaming into the ether body becomes visible. In these flashes thought still *lives*. Upon awakening it is captured by the forces through which it dies, becomes shadow. This connection between dreaming and waking thoughts is meaningful. Man *thinks* with the same forces by which he grows and lives. Yet these forces must die in order for him to become a thinker.

This is the point where a correct understanding can arise as to why man grasps reality through thinking. In his thoughts he has the dead picture of what creates him from quickening reality.

The dead picture: this dead picture is, however, the result of the activity of the great painter, the cosmos itself. To be sure, there is no life in it. If life were in it, the I could not unfold. But it contains the universe's whole content in all its glory. To the extent possible at the time, in my *Philosophy of Freedom* I described this inner connection between thinking and reality. It is where I wrote that a bridge leads from the profundity of thinking to the profundity of nature's reality.

For normal consciousness sleep extinguishes because it leads to the earth's sprouting life in the becoming macrocosm. When imaginative consciousness eliminates this extinguishing process, an earth with the sharp contours of the mineral, vegetable and animals kingdoms no longer stands before the human soul. Rather is it a living process which kindles within the earth and flames out into the macrocosm. In the waking state man, with his own I-being, must withdraw from the world-being in order to achieve free self-

138

consciousness. In the sleeping state he reunites with the world-being.

During the present cosmic moment the rhythm of man's earthly existence consists of experiencing his own Being outside the "inner" world; and the extinguishing of the consciousness of his own Being within the "inner" world.

During the time between death and a new birth the human I lives within the Beings of the spirit-world. There everything which escaped consciousness during the earthly waking state enters this consciousness. The macrocosmic forces emerge from their completely living existence during the remote past up until their moribund condition in the present. The earthly forces also emerge however, which are the seeds of the becoming macrocosm. And while sleeping man sees into it as clearly as he sees the earth glistening in the sun during his earth life.

Only insofar as the macrocosm has become moribund, as it is at present, can the human being go through life between death and a new birth with a higher wakefulness than during his waking earth life. An awakening through which man becomes capable of mastering *the* forces which are present only fleetingly in dreams. *These* forces fill the whole cosmos. They are all-pervading. The human being derives from them the impulses from which the great artwork of the macrocosm, his body, is formed during his descent to earth.

What dawns sun-abandoned in dreams lives in the spirit-world spiritually sundrenched, waiting, till the Beings of the higher hierarchies or man invoke it to creative activity.

Goetheanum, January 1925

156. In the waking state, in order to experience *himself* in completely free self-consciousness, man must renounce experiencing the true essence of reality in his own being and in that of nature. He raises himself out of the ocean of this reality in order to truly experience his own I in the thought-shadows.

157. In the sleeping state, man lives with the earth's surroundings; but this life extinguishes his self-consciousness.

158. In dreams the powerful universal being flares up in semi-consciousness — from which the human being is woven and from which he forms his body during his descent from the spirit-world. In earthly life this powerful universal being dies out in man, even as far as the thought-shadows, for only in this way that it can become the foundation for his self-consciousness.

Gnosis and Anthroposophy

When the Mystery of Golgotha took place, "Gnosis" was the manner of thinking of a part of humanity who could provide not merely a feeling but also a cognitive understanding of the event which had the greatest impact in the earthly history of mankind.

If one wishes to understand the mentality of those in whom Gnosis was prevalent it is necessary to bear in mind that the age of Gnosis was that of the Comprehension or Sensitivity Soul. Due to this fact one can also find the reason for the almost complete disappearance of Gnosis from history. This disappearance is perhaps one of the strangest occurrences in human evolution.

The unfolding of the Comprehension or Sensitivity Soul was preceded by that of the Sentient Soul and the latter was preceded by that of the sentient body. When world events were perceived through the sentient body, all human knowledge was in the senses. The world was perceived in colors, tones and so forth; but in the colors, tones and warmth states a world of spiritual beings was conceived. One didn't speak about "matter" in which colors, warmth states and so forth appeared; one spoke of spiritual beings which were revealed by what the senses perceived.

The unfolding of "comprehension", which later lived in man alongside sense perception, did not yet exist in that age. Either one concentrated on the outer world, in which case the gods revealed themselves to him through his senses, or his soul withdrew from the outer world and he felt a faint sense of life within him.

A meaningful transition took place when the Sentient Soul developed. The manifestation of the divine through the senses diminished. In its place appeared the more or less divine-less sense impressions, the color and warmth states, etc. In man's interior the divine revealed itself in spiritual form, in pictorial ideas. Thus he perceived the world from two sides: from outside through sense impressions, from within through impressions of spiritual ideas.

Man then had to be able to perceive the spirit-impressions in as clear and as defined a form as he previously had perceived the divine through the senses. He could do so as long as the Sentient Soul age persisted. From his inner being pictorial ideas rose up fully formed. From within he was filled with sense-free spiritual content, which was a mirror of cosmic-content. The gods who previously appeared to him clothed in the senses now appeared in spiritual garments.

This was the age when Gnosis arose and lived. A marvelous cognition existed in which one could participate if he developed his inner self in purity in order that divine content could manifest itself. From the fourth and into the first millennium before the Mystery of Golgotha this Gnosis prevailed in the most knowledgeably advanced portion of humanity.

Then the age of the Comprehension or Sensitivity Soul began. The pictures of the divine world no longer emerged on their own from the human being's inner self. He had to use inner strength in order to draw them out of his soul. The outer world with its sense impressions became questionable. Only when he used inner strength to draw the divine world-pictures from his soul did he obtain answers.

But the pictures were pale compared to their previous form. This was the mental constitution of the humanity which developed so wonderfully in Greece. The Greek felt himself to be in the sensible outer world and felt in it a magical strength as an impetus for the unfolding of cosmic images. In philosophy this mental constitution developed in Platonism.

But behind it all stood the Mysteries, in which what existed from the age of the Sentient Soul in Gnosis was faithfully preserved. Human souls were trained for this faithful preservation. In normal evolution the Comprehension or Sensitivity Soul developed. Through special training the Sentient Soul was revivified. Thus during the Comprehension or Sensitivity Soul Age a richly developed world of the Mysteries existed. In this world lived the cosmic images of the gods, also insofar as they included rituals. One looks into the interior of these Mysteries and views the universe in the images of the most wonderful ritualistic acts.

Those who experienced *that* also perceived the Mystery of Golgotha, when it took place, in its most profound cosmic significance. But the Mysteries were kept completely apart from the outer world's disorder in order to maintain the purity of the world of spiritual images. And for human souls this became ever more difficult. Then spiritual beings descended from the spiritual cosmos into the highest Mystery sites in order to help those who were striving for knowledge. In this way the impulses of the Sentient Soul age unfolded further under the influence of the "gods" themselves. A Mystery-Gnosis arose, about which only a few had the barest notion. Beside it existed what could be absorbed by means of the Comprehension or Sensitivity Soul. This was exoteric Gnosis, remnants of which have come down to posterity.

In esoteric Gnosis, people became less able to raise themselves to the unfolding of the Sentient Soul. This esoteric wisdom gradually became the sole possession of the "gods". And this is a secret of the historical evolution of humanity: that from the first Christian centuries until the middle ages "divine mysteries" were active in it. In these "divine mysteries" angelic beings preserved for human beings what they could no longer preserve themselves. Thus Mystery-Gnosis persevered while exoteric Gnosis was being eradicated.

The *Cosmic-Picture-Content,* which in the Mystery-Gnosis was preserved in a spiritual way by spiritual beings as long as it was to be active in human evolution, could not be grasped by conscious human understanding. But its feeling content was to be preserved, and in the right cosmic moment it was to be given to the people who were prepared for it, in order that by means of its soul-warmth the Consciousness Soul could penetrate later into the spirit realm in a new way. Thus spiritual beings built the bridge between the old and the new cosmic contents.

Indications of this secret about human evolution exist. The sacred Jasper cup of the Grail which Christ used when he broke bread and in which Joseph of Arimathea caught the blood from Christ's wounds, therewith containing the Mystery of

Golgotha, was — according to the legend — taken into custody by angels until Titurel could build the Grail Castle and let it descend to the human beings prepared to receive it.

Spiritual beings bore the Cosmic-Pictures in which the secrets of Golgotha lived. They sank the feeling content (not the picture-content, for that was not possible) into humanity when the appropriate time arrived. This implanting of the feeling-content of ancient knowledge can be only a stimulus, but a most powerful stimulus, which in our age of the Consciousness Soul, and in light of Michael's activity, can develop a completely new understanding of the Mystery of Golgotha.

Anthroposophy strives for this new understanding. From the foregoing description one sees that it cannot be a renewal of Gnosis, which depended on the kind of knowledge derived from the Sentient Soul for its content; but that it [anthroposophy] must bring an equally rich content from the Consciousness Soul in a completely new way.

Goetheanum, January, 1925

159. Gnosis developed in its true form during the Sentient Soul age (fourth to first millennium before the Mystery of Golgotha). The "divine" revealed itself to human beings during this age as spirit-content within them, whereas during the previous age of the sentient body it manifested itself through the sense impressions of the outer world.

160. During the age of the Comprehension or Sensitivity Soul, the spirit-content of the "divine" could only be faintly experienced. Gnosis was preserved in strict Mysteries, and when men were no longer able to do this because they were not able to revivify the Sentient Soul, up until the Middle Ages it was accomplished by spiritual beings — although not the cognitive, but the feeling content. (the Grail legend contains intimations of this.) Meanwhile exoteric Gnosis, which penetrated into the Comprehension or Sensitivity Soul, was exterminated.

161. Anthroposophy cannot be a renewal of Gnosis, for the latter was dependent on the development of the Sentient Soul. Anthroposophy must, in the light of Michael's activity, develop a new understanding of the world and Christ derived from the Consciousness Soul. Gnosis was a cognition preserved from an ancient age, and was the best way for humanity to understand the Mystery of Golgotha when it actually occurred.

Human Freedom and the Age of Michael

In the human capacity for memory lies the personal image of a cosmic force which has affected humanity in the way described in the previous contemplation. This cosmic force is still active however. It acts as a force for growth, as a vivifying impulse in the background of human life. It is mostly active there. Only a smaller portion is set aside to act on the Consciousness Soul. There it acts as a force for remembrance.

It is necessary to see this remembrance force in the right light. When in the present epoch of cosmic evolution man perceives with the senses, this perception is a momentary illumination of world-*pictures* in his consciousness. The illumination comes when the senses are directed towards the outer world; it illumines consciousness; it disappears when the senses are no longer directed towards the outer world. This illumination in the human mind must not have duration. For if it did man could not remove it from his consciousness quickly enough; he would lose himself in [the quantity of] his consciousness-contents. He would no longer be him*self.* Only for a short time, in the so-called after-images, which so interested Goethe, may the illumination by perception last in consciousness. Nor may this consciousness content solidify into being; it must remain pictorial. It may become as little real as the image in a mirror can become real. Man would lose himself in something that lived fully in his consciousness as reality, as much as he would in something that had duration of its own. He could not be him*self* in that case either.

The perception by the senses of the outer world is an inner painting by the human soul. A painting without material substance. A painting in spiritual becoming and spiritual elapsing. Just as a rainbow comes into being, then disappears without leaving a trace, a perception comes into being and disappears without *it* leaving, by its own nature, a memory behind.

But at the same time, with *every* perception something else happens between the human soul and the outer world — one which lies in a more concealed part of the soul, where the forces of growth, where the life impulses act. In *this* part of the soul not only a fleeting image is engraved by perception, but an enduring, real one. Man can endure this for it is coherent with his Being as content of the world. When this happens he can no more lose himself as when he grows and nourishes himself without full consciousness.

When man retrieves his memories from within, it is an inner perception of what remained in this second process of perception of the outer world. Once again the soul paints a picture, but now he paints the living events contained in his own inner being. Again no lasting reality may remain in his *consciousness,* but only the forming and vanishing of a picture. In this way the thoughts formed through perception and remembering them are connected in the human soul.

But the remembrance forces continually strive to be more than can they can be if man is not to lose him *self* as a self-conscious being. For the remembrance forces are the remains of past human evolution and as such come into the sphere of Lucifer's power. Lucifer strives to solidify the outer world's impressions in the human being to the extent that they continually illumine as thoughts in his consciousness.

This Luciferic striving would be crowned with success if the Michael-Force did not counteract it. This latter force does not allow what has been painted with inner light to solidify into Being, but maintains it as emerging and disappearing pictures. However, the excessive force which is pressured out of the human being by Lucifer will be transformed into imaginative force during the Michael Age. For the force of imagination will gradually enter into the general intellectual human consciousness. But this will not burden humanity with enduring realities in its present consciousness, which will continue to act with emerging and disappearing images. With his imaginations he will tower above in a higher spiritual world, just as he delves down into his true humanity through his memories. Man does not retain the imaginations within him; they are recorded in the cosmos, from whence he is always able to copy them into his picture-thinking.

In this way what Michael safeguards from solidifying in man's inner life is absorbed by the spiritual world. What humanity experiences through the forces of conscious imagining becomes, at the same time, a content of that world. That this can happen is a result of the Mystery of Golgotha. The Christ-Force impregnates human imagination into the cosmos. The Christ-Force that is conjoined with the earth. As long as it was not conjoined with the earth, but acted on the earth from without as solar force, the growth and life impulses entered into humanity's inner being. Man was formed and preserved from out the cosmos. Since the Christ impulse lives in the earth, man is being returned to the cosmos in his self-consciousness.

Humanity, originally a cosmic being, became an earthly being. He is therefore disposed to become a cosmic being once again, once he has become *himself* as an earthly being.

In this fact, that man in his momentary conceptions [or mental pictures] does not live in being, but only in a reflection of being, in a picture-being, lies the possibility of achieving freedom. All being in consciousness is coercive. Only the *image* cannot coerce. If something happens due to [the influence of] its impression, it must happen independently *of it*. Man becomes free by elevating himself by his Consciousness Soul out of being and emerging in the *non-being* of picture consciousness.

Thereby an important question arises: Does man lose his own being by leaving a part of his essence and plunging into non-being? This is again a point where one stands before a great riddle when contemplating the world.

What is experienced in the consciousness as a representation [or mental picture] arises out of the cosmos. In respect to this cosmos, man plunges into non-being. He frees himself in his representations from all cosmic forces. He "paints" the cosmos while outside it.

If it were *only* so, freedom would flash up for a cosmic instant in the human being; but in the same instant he would melt away as a human essence. However, because he becomes free of the cosmos in his representations, in his unconscious mind he is connected to his previous earth lives and the lives between death and a new birth. As a conscious individual he is in a picture-existence, and he remains in his unconscious mind in spiritual reality. While he experiences freedom in his *present* I, his *past* I keeps his being intact.

In respect to Being, in his representations man is completely devoted to what he has become through the cosmic and earthly past existence. This indicates the abyss of the *nothing* over which man leaps in human evolution when he becomes a free being. Michael's activity and the Christ impulse make the leap possible.

Goetheanum, January 1925

162. In his representations [mental pictures] man does not live with his consciousness in being, but in pictorial being, in non-being. He is thereby *freed* from mutual experience with the cosmos. Images do not coerce. Only being coerces.

163. In the moment of such a representation [mental picture], man is connected with the world's being only by what he has become from the past: his previous earth lives and his lives between death and new birth.

164. This cosmic leap over non-being can only be accomplished through Michael's activity and the Christ impulse.

Man as a Thinking and Remembering Being

With his representations (thinking) and the experiencing of memories, man finds himself within the physical world. However, no matter where he looks with his senses in the physical world, nowhere does he find what gives him the strength to form mental pictures [representations] and to remember.

Self-consciousness appears in thinking. This is — in the sense of our previous considerations — an acquisition which man has from the earth forces. But *these* earthly forces remain hidden to the senses. In earthly life man thinks about what the senses impart; but the force to think does not come from what he thinks about in this way.

Where does this earthly force come from which forms the mental pictures (thinking) and the memory pictures? It is found when one looks back with spiritual vision at what man brings with him from previous earth lives. Normal consciousness does not know this. It lives in humanity unconsciously at first. It manifests itself when, after his spiritual existence, man comes to earth, where he is instantly connected to the earthly forces which do not fall within the realm of sense observation and thinking. Man is not in this realm with representations (thinking), but with the will, which acts in accordance with destiny.

In this respect, one may speak of the forces contained in the earth which fall outside the realm of the senses as the "spiritual earth" — the opposite pole to the physical one. It therefore follows that man lives in and with the "spiritual earth" as a willing being, and that as a representing (thinking) one, although he is within the physical earth, as such he does not live *with* it.

As a thinking being, man carries forces from the spirit-world into the physical one; but he remains a spirit-being with these forces, who only *appears* in the physical world, but does not enter into commonality with it.

The representing (thinking) human being has commonality only with the "spiritual earth" during his earthly sojourn. And it is from *this* commonality that his self-consciousness matures. It is therefore thanks to spiritual processes during earthly life that self-consciousness appears.

If these processes are observed with spiritual vision, one envisions the "human I". One comes to the realm of the human astral body via the experience of remembrance. By remembering, not merely the results of previous earth lives stream into the present I, which is the case with representation (thinking), but forces from the spirit-world, which one experiences between death and a new birth, stream into man's inner being. This streaming is directed to the astral body.

Within the physical earth there is no place for the direct reception of these instreaming forces. As a being who remembers, man cannot unite with the things and events that he perceives with his senses, just as he is unable to unite with them as a thinking being.

But he does achieve commonality with what transforms the physical into processes and events, although it is not physical itself. These are the rhythmical processes in nature and man. Day and night alternate rhythmically in nature, the seasons follow each other rhythmically, and so on. In humans breathing and blood circulation are rhythmic, as are sleeping and waking.

Rhythmical processes are not physical in nature or in man. They could be called half-spiritual. The physical as thing disappears in the rhythmical process. By remembering, man is transferred to *his* and to nature's rhythmical processes. He lives in his astral body.

Indian yoga would completely evaporate in rhythmical experience. It would abandon the area of thinking, the I, and in inner experience, similar to memory, look into the world which lies behind what normal consciousness can know.

Western spiritual life may not suppress the I in order to gain knowledge. It must accompany the I to spiritual perception. This can't happen if one pushes so hard from the sensitive to the rhythmical world that one only experiences in the rhythmical the half-spiritual nature of the physical. One must rather find *that* sphere of the spirit-world which manifests itself in the rhythmical.

Therefore two things are possible. First: while experiencing the physical in the rhythmical, confirm how this physical becomes half-spiritual. This is an older path, no longer to be trodden today. Second: experiencing the spirit-world which has as its sphere cosmic rhythms within and outside man, just as man has the earth and its physical beings and processes.

To *this* spirit-world belongs everything which happens through Michael in the present cosmic moment. A spirit such as Michael brings what would otherwise lie in the Luciferic region into purely human evolution — which is not influenced by Lucifer — in that he chooses the rhythmical world as his dwelling place.

This can all be envisioned once man enters into Imagination.[1] For the soul lives in rhythm with Imagination; and Michael's world manifests itself in rhythm. Remembrance, memory is already within this world, but not yet in depth. Normal consciousness experiences nothing of this. By entering Imagination, however, the world of subjective remembrance emerges at first from the rhythmical world; it passes at once to the primal images (Urbilder), living in the etheric, created by the divine-spiritual world for the physical world.

For one experiences the radiant cosmic pictures of the creation of worlds concealed in the ether. And the sun forces weaving in this ether: they do not merely radiate, they invoke cosmic primal images from the light. The sun appears as the cosmic painter of the universe. It is the cosmic counterpart of the impulses which paint representational (thought) pictures in man.

Goetheanum, January 1925

[1] The author is referring here (I think) to the first of the three stages of initiation: 1) imagination, 2) inspiration, 3) intuition. (translator).

165. Man lives as a thinking being in the earth's domain; However, he does not enter into commonality with it. As spirit-being he lives in such a way that he perceives what is physical; but he receives the forces for thinking from the "spiritual earth", in the same way in which he experiences destiny as the result of previous earth lives.

166. What in remembrance (memories) is experienced is already in the world where the physical becomes half-spiritual in rhythm and where such spirit-processes take place as those which occur through Michael in the present cosmic moment.

167. Whoever learns to know thinking and remembering correctly understands how man as an earthly being lives within the earthly realm, but does not entirely submerge his being into this realm; but as an outer-earthly being seeks his self-consciousness, as the consummation of his I, through commonality with the "spiritual earth".

The Macrocosmic Nature of Man

At first the cosmos reveals itself to man from the earthly and the outer-earthly side, the world of the stars [heavenly bodies — trans.] Man feels himself related to the earth and its forces. Life teaches him very clearly about *this* relationship. *In contemporary times*, however, he doesn't feel related to the stars in the same way. But this is the case only as long as he is not conscious of his etheric body. Grasping the etheric body in imaginations develops a feeling of belonging to the world of stars, just as one has such a feeling about the earth through consciousness of the physical body.

The forces that place the etheric body in the world come from the *periphery* of the universe, while those for the physical body stream from the *center* of the earth.

But together with the etheric forces which stream into the earth from the periphery of the cosmos, come the cosmic impulses which act in the astral bodies of men.

The ether is like a sea in which the astral forces swim, approaching the earth from all the diverse cosmic directions.

In the present cosmic age, only the mineral and vegetable kingdoms are able to have a direct connection to the astral forces which stream to the earth on the waves of the ether. Not, however, the animal kingdom or humanity.

Spiritual vision shows that in the case of the animal kingdom it is not the present astral forces which stream into the embryonic stage, but those which did so during the Ancient Moon period.

In the vegetable kingdom one sees how the wonderfully manifold forms are structured when the astral severs itself from the ether and acts on the plant world.

With respect to the animal kingdom, one sees how the astrality that was active during the Ancient Moon period and was derived from the spiritual, has been preserved and as such remains in the spirit-world and does not enter the etheric world. The effectiveness of *this* astrality is mediated by the moon forces, which have also remained at the previous stage of the earth's evolution.

In the animal kingdom we therefore have the result of impulses which manifested themselves in an natural way in the earth's previous stage, whereas in the present cosmic age they have withdrawn to the spirit-world, which actively streams through the earth. Spiritual vision observes that within the animal kingdom, in the penetration of the physical and etheric bodies by the astral body at present, only the astral forces preserved from the past are meaningful. Once the animal has its astral body however, then the sun-impulses enter actively into it. The sun forces cannot give the animal astrality; once in the animal, however, they are necessarily active in its growth, nutrition and so forth.

For humanity it is different. It also receives at first its astrality from the preserved Moon forces. But the sun forces contain astral impulses which remain ineffective for the animal kingdom, but continue to affect human astrality in the same way as when the Moon forces first imbued humanity with astrality.

In the animal astral body one sees the moon world; in the human astral body one sees the harmonious concordance of the sun and moon worlds. It is due to this sun effect in the human astral body that man is able to absorb what streams spiritually from the earth for the development of his self-consciousness.

Astrality streams forth from the *periphery* of the universe. It acts either as what presently streams forth, or what streamed forth in the past and is preserved. However, everything which relates to the formation of the I as the vehicle of selfconsciousness must stream out from the *center* of a star. Astrality acts from the periphery, what is relevant to the I acts from a center. The earth as a heavenly body gives impulse to the human I from its center. Forces stream from the center of every star [heavenly body] from which the I of some being is formed.

This indicates the polarity between a *star's [heavenly body's] center* and the *cosmic periphery*.

One sees from this description how the animal kingdom still exists today as a result of earlier earthly evolutionary forces, how it uses up the preserved astral forces, how it must, however, disappear once these forces are used up. On the other hand, with man new astral forces are created from the sun, which enables him to continue his evolution into the future.

Without being conscious of man's relationship to the stars as well as to the earth, it is not possible to understand the essence of humanity. And what man receives from the earth for his self-consciousness also derives from the spirit-world which acts within the earth. That the sun gives to man what his astrality needs derives from the activity which took place during the ancient Sun period. The earth received there the capacity to develop humanity's I-impulses. It is the spiritual from that period which the earth preserved of the Sun forces, and which is preserved from dying out now through the present activity of the sun.

The earth was once itself Sun. It was spiritualized. In the present cosmic age the sun acts from without. This continuously rejuvenates the aging spiritual forces from ancient times. For what continues to act without absorbing the forces of the present succumbs to the Luciferic.

One can say that the man's feeling for his connection to the outer-earthly cosmos is so muted in this cosmic epoch that he doesn't notice it within his consciousness. And it is not merely muted, it is drowned out by feeling connected to the earth. Because man must find his self-consciousness in the earth, he grew so attached to it at the beginning of the Consciousness Soul age that it acts much more strongly on him than is appropriate for the correct course of his soul life. He is to a certain extent *benumbed* by the impressions of the world of the senses. Because of this numbness he does not actualize the free thinking of which he is capable.

The whole epoch from the middle of the nineteenth century on was such a benumbing through sense impressions. The great illusion of this age is that man took the overly strong life of the senses to be the correct one — the life of the senses which strove to extinguish the life in the outer-earthly cosmos. The Ahrimanic powers were able to unfold their being within this benumbing. Lucifer was held back more by the sun forces than was Ahriman, who was able to call forth, especially in scientifically inclined people, the dangerous feeling that ideas are only applicable to sense impressions. Therefore anthroposophy can find little understanding in those circles. One stands before the results of spiritual knowledge and tries to understand them with ideas. But these ideas do not grasp the spiritual, because they are benumbed by Ahrimanic knowledge through the senses. And thus one fears that he will succumb to blind belief in authority if he is open to the results of the spiritual seer's research.

The outer-earthly cosmos became ever darker for human consciousness during the second half of the nineteenth century.

If man is again able to vivify the ideas within him, even when they are not supported by the world of the senses, then light will stream back to his gaze from the outer-earthly cosmos. But this means recognizing Michael in his realm. Once the Michael festival in autumn becomes true and internal, then those who participate in the festival will experience the following as a leitmotiv which will live in their consciousness: *Idea filled, the soul experiences spirit-light when the sense revelations only echo in man as remembrances.*

If man can experience this, then, after the festival, he will be able to submerge again in the right way into the sense world. And Ahriman will not be able to harm him.

Goetheanum, January 1925

168. At the beginning of the Consciousness Soul age a dampening of the human feeling of connection with the outer-earthly cosmos took place. In contrast thereto, the feeling of connection to the earth by experiencing sense impressions was so strong, especially among scientifically inclined people, that a benumbing resulted.

169. Within this benumbing, the Ahrimanic powers work so dangerously that man lives in the illusion that this strong benumbing experience is the correct one and constitutes real evolutionary progress.

170. Man must find the strength to enlighten his world of ideas and experience them as such, also when they are not supported by the benumbed sense-world. In this experience of the independently enlightened world of ideas the feeling of connection to the outer-earthly cosmos will awaken. The basis for Michael festivals will then exist.

The Sensing and Thinking Organization of Humanity in Relation to the World

When man observes his own humanity using imaginative cognition, he initially eliminates his sensing system from this vision. For his self-observation he becomes a being without this system. He doesn't cease to have images before his mind which were previously conveyed by the sense organs; but he does cease to feel connected to the physical world through these organs: this direct observation is a proof that man — beyond sense perception — is also connected to the natural world in another way not dependent upon the senses. It is a connection with the spirit which is incorporated in the natural outer world.

In this kind of vision, the physical world falls away from the viewer. It is the earthly which falls away. Man feels the earth as no longer a part of him. One could assume that self-consciousness is thus obliterated — something which seems to follow from the previous considerations — that self-consciousness is a result of man's connection to the earth. But that is not the case. What he acquired through earthly means remains with him, even when he divests himself of it *after acquiring* it, through active conscious cognition.

This spiritual-imaginative vision reveals that man has not actually bound himself to the sensing system intensively. It is not *he* who lives in this sensing system, but the environment, which has built *itself* with its essence into the sense organization of man.

And the imaginatively seeing person therefore also considers the sensing organization as a part of the outer world. A part of the outer world which, however, is closer to him than the natural environment, but is nevertheless outer world. It differs from the ordinary outer world only in that man can only immerse himself in the latter through knowledge obtained by sense observation. He does, however, immerse himself in this world. The sense organization is outer world, but man reaches into this outer word with his spirit-soul essence, which he brings with him from the spirit-world when he enters into earthly existence.

Except for the fact that the human being fills his sensing organization with his spirit-soul essence, this organization is [part of] the outer world, just as the plant world which surrounds him is. The eye, after all, belongs to the world, not to the person, just as the rose which he perceives belongs to the world and not to him.

In the age of cosmic evolution which man has just passed through, thinkers appeared who said that colors, tones and sensations of warmth are not in the world, but in people. The "color red", they say, is not outside in the environment, but is only the effect on man of something unknown. But the truth is just the opposite of this opinion. It is not color and the eye which belong to the human being, but the eye along with color which belong to the world. During his earth life man does not let earthly surroundings stream into him; rather he *grows outward* into this outer world between birth and death.

It is significant that at the end of the dark age, in which man gazed out at the world without an inkling of the light of the spirit, the correct concept of man's relation to his environment was exactly the opposite of what is true.

When by means of imaginative cognition man has shed the environment in which he lives with his senses, another organization enters his experience, of which *thinking* is a function, as picture perception is a function of the senses. And now man knows that he is connected to the cosmic stellar environment through his thinking organization, just as he was previously connected to the earthly environment through the senses. He realizes that he is a cosmic being. His thoughts are no longer shadowy images; they are saturated with reality, as are those obtained by sense perception.

If he then advances to Inspiration, he becomes aware that this world, which is supported by his thinking-organization, can also be shed, as was the earthly one. He realizes that by this thinking-organization he doesn't belong to his own being either, but to the world. He realizes how the cosmic thoughts reverberate in his own thinking-organization. And he becomes aware that he does not think by taking in images from the world, but by *growing out* into the cosmic thoughts with his thinking-organization.

Both with respect to his sense-organization as well as his thinking-system, man is *world*. The world builds itself within him. Neither in sense perception nor in thinking is he himself, but he is world-content.

Into his thinking-organization man extends the spirit-soul of his being, which belongs neither to the earthly nor to the stellar world, but is of a purely spiritual nature and continues in the human being from earth life to earth life. This spirit-soul nature is accessible only to Inspiration. Thus through his Inspiration man steps out of his earthly-cosmic organization in order to stand before himself as a purely spirit-soul being. In this pure spirit-soul existence man meets the expression of his destiny.

With the sense-organization man lives in his physical body, with the thinking-organization in his etheric body. After shedding both organizations by means of experienced cognition, he is in his astral body.

Every time the human being sheds something from his acquired being, on the *one* hand although his soul-content becomes poorer, on the other hand at the same time it becomes richer. Although after shedding the physical body the beauty of the plant kingdom perceptible to his senses has paled, in its stead the world of elementary beings who live in the plant kingdom appear before his soul.

Because this is the case, an ascetic mood does not dominate the person with real spiritual knowledge in respect to what the senses perceive. In *spiritual experience* he retains the need to perceive the spiritually experienced again through sense perception. And as the complete man strives to experience reality as a whole, sense perception awakens the desire for the opposite pole — the world of elementary beings. Similarly, the vision of the elementary beings again awakens the desire for the content of sense perception.

In a full human life, the spirit has need for the senses, and the senses for the spirit. Spiritual existence would be empty if there were no memory of the experience of sense experience; Sense experience would be in darkness if the force of spiritual light did not enter into it, albeit subconsciously at first.

Therefore, when the person has become sufficiently mature to experience Michael's activity, an impoverishment of the soul in respect to experiencing nature does not occur, rather the contrary: enrichment. And his feelings do not tend to disengage from sense experiences, but a joyful disposition exists to absorb the wonders of the world of the senses.

Goetheanum, February, 1925

171. The human sense-organization does not belong to the being of man, rather is it incorporated into him from the environment during his earth life. The perceiving eye is spatially located in man, but essentially it is *in the world.* And man reaches with his spirit-soul into what the world experiences in him through his senses. And he does not take in the physical environment during his earthly life, but grows into it with his spirit-soul being.

172. It is similar with the thinking-organization. Man grows by means of it into the stellar world. He recognizes himself as stellar world. He lives and moves within cosmic thoughts when he has shed the sensing-organization in experienced cognition.

173. After shedding both, the earthly and the stellar worlds, man stands before himself as a spirit-soul being. For he is no longer *world,* but human in the true sense of the word. And to be conscious of what he experiences here is called *self-knowledge*, as being conscious in the sensing and thinking organization is called *world-knowledge*.

Memory and Conscience

In the sleeping state man is devoted to the cosmos. He brings to the cosmos the results of previous earth lives when he descends from the spirit-soul world to the earth. He withdraws this content of his humanity from the cosmos when awake.

Devotion to the cosmos and withdrawal from the cosmos is the rhythm between birth and death.

The withdrawal of the human spirit-soul from the cosmos is at the same time a reception of same by the senses-nervous organization. The physical and life processes are united with the human spirit-soul for unified activity when in the waking state. Sense perception, formation of memory pictures and imagination are contained in this activity. These activities are bound to the physical body. The representations, the thinking in which man becomes *conscious* of what takes place semi-consciously in perception, imagination and memory are bound to the thinking organization.

In this same thinking organization lies the field through which man experiences his self-consciousness. The thinking organization is a stellar-organization. If it lived out its existence *as such* alone, then man would have no self-consciousness, but a gods-consciousness. But the thinking organization is a stellar-organization drawn out of the stars-cosmos and transferred to earthly occurrence. Man becomes a self-conscious being when experiencing the stellar world on earth. This, therefore, is the field of man's inner life in which the divine-spiritual world, which is bound to man, releases him in order than he can become human in the full sense of the word.

But immediately beneath the thinking organization, where sense perception, imagination and memories take place, the divine-spiritual world *lives together* with humanity. One can say that in the unfolding of memory the divine-spiritual lives in man's waking state. The other two activities — sense perception and imagination — are only modifications of the formation of memory pictures. The inception of memory pictures originates in sense perception; in the substance of imagination what is retained of this substance illuminates the soul.

The sleeping state carries man's spirit-soul out into the cosmos. He is immersed into the divine-spiritual cosmos by this activity of his astral body and his I. He is not only beyond the physical world, but also beyond the stellar world. But he is within the divine-spiritual beings through whom his existence originated.

In the present time of cosmic evolution these divine-spiritual beings act in such a way that they instill the moral cosmic essence in the astral body and the I during the sleeping state. All the cosmic occurrences in the sleeping person are real moral occurrences, and have nothing at all to do with what occurs in nature.

Man carries these occurrences as aftereffects from the sleeping into the waking state. The aftereffects themselves remain in the sleeping state. For man is only awake in the life which tends towards thinking. What is happening in the willing sphere during the waking state is wrapped in dullness such as during sleep the *whole* soul is. But the divine-spiritual continues to weave in this dullness of will in the waking state. The human being is morally as good or as bad as he can be according to how close he can come to the divine-spiritual when sleeping. And he comes closer or remains distant according to the moral direction of his previous earth lives.

From the depths of the waking soul's being resounds during sleep — together with the divine-spiritual world — what is able to be implanted in this soul. *What resounds is the voice of conscience.* This shows that whereas the materialistic viewpoint is mostly inclined to explain things based on nature, spiritual cognition sides with morality. In *memory* the divine-spiritual essence acts directly on the waking human being; in *conscience* this divine-spiritual essence acts indirectly — as aftereffect — in the waking human being.

Memory formation occurs in the nervous-senses organization; Conscience formation occurs as a purely soul-spiritual process, but in the metabolic-limbs organization. Between these lies the rhythmic organization. Its activity is cultivated on two sides as a polarity. In its breathing rhythm it has an intimate relation to sense perception and thinking. In lung-breathing the process is coarsest; it becomes ever finer until, as a refined breathing process, it is sense perception and thinking. Sense perception is very close to breathing — but breathing by the sense-organs, not by the lungs. More distant from lung-breathing and supported by the thinking organization, is representation, thinking; and what borders on the rhythm of blood circulation — an inner breathing which is bound to the metabolic-limbs organization — is revealed as imaginative activity. This extends, psychologically, into the willing sphere, as the circulatory rhythm extends into the metabolic-limbs organization.

In imaginative activity the thinking organization approaches the willing organization. It is a submerging of the waking person into the sleeping sphere of his will. In the case of people who are developed in this way, the contents of the mind appear like dreams in the waking state. Goethe was organized in such a way. Thus he told Schiller that he should interpret his poetic dreams for him. A different organization was active in Schiller. He lived from what he brought with him from his previous earth lives. He had to seek imaginative substance with a strong will.

For its overall intentions, the Ahrimanic power counts on those people who are disposed to imagination, whose sense perception seems to develop into imaginative pictures on its own. With the help of such people, this power hopes to completely sunder the evolution of humanity from the past and point it in the direction *it* wants. Luciferic power counts on those people who are organized towards the willing sphere, who strongly transform sense perceptions into imaginative pictures through love for ideology (Weltanschauung). Through such people it would like to completely maintain human evolution within the impulses of the past. In this way it could prevent mankind from submerging into the sphere where the Ahrimanic power must be overcome.

On earth man stands between two opposite poles. Above him the stars are spread. From them radiate the forces related to everything which is calculable and regularity on earth: regular changes from day to night, seasons, longer cosmic periods — they are the earthly reflection of stellar processes.

The other pole radiates from the interior of the earth. Irregularity works in it: wind and weather, thunder and lightning, earthquakes, volcanic eruptions reflect this inner earthly process.

The human being is an image of this stellar-earthly state of being. The stellar order lives in his thinking organization, earthly chaos in his metabolic-limbs organization. In the rhythmic organization the earthly human being experiences himself in free equilibrium.

Goetheanum, February 1925

174. The human being is spiritually-physically organized from two sides. Firstly from the physical-etheric cosmos. What streams into *this* organization from the divine-spiritual essence lives in it as the forces of sense perception, the capacity for memory and imaginative activity.

175. Secondly man is organized according to his previous earth lives. This organization is completely soul-spiritual and lives in him through his astral body and his I. What lives as divine-spiritual essence in this human essence radiates as the voice of conscience and everything associated with it.

176. In his rhythmic organization man has the continuous unifying of the two sides by divine-spiritual impulses. By the experiencing of rhythm the force of memory is carried to the will, and the power of conscience into the realm of ideas.

The Supposed Extinguishing of Spiritual Knowledge in Modern Times

In order to correctly judge Anthroposophy in its relation to the evolution of the Consciousness Soul, one must again observe the spiritual constitution of civilized humanity, which began with the advent of natural science and reached its peak in the nineteenth century, and compare its character with that of previous ages. In the [previous] ages of conscious evolution of humanity, knowledge was seen as what brought man together with the spirit-world. Knowledge was considered to be what related man to spirit. In art and religion knowledge *lived*.

This changed with the advent of the Consciousness Soul. Knowledge began to have little to do with a large part of human soul-life. It was used to investigate the development of man's relation to existence when he concentrated his senses and his intellectual judgment toward "nature". But people no longer wanted to use it to determine how man develops his relation to the spirit-world when he uses his capacity for inner perception as opposed to his senses.

Thus the necessity arose to associate human spiritual life to past knowledge, to tradition, instead of to the present. Human soul life was torn in two. Striving for knowledge of nature in the present was the goal on the one hand. On the other hand was the experience of a relation to the spiritual world, from which knowledge flowed from olden times. All understanding of how *this* relation came about in previous times was gradually lost. Humanity possessed the tradition, but no longer the way in which the traditional truths had *become known*. One could only *believe* in the tradition.

Someone who considered the spiritual situation around the middle of the nineteenth century with complete presence of mind, would have to recognize that humanity had come to the point where it could only be considered capable of developing cognition which had nothing to do with the spirit. Humanity of previous times was able to investigate the spirit; however, the capacity for this kind of investigation had been lost. The consequences of this attitude was not taken into account. Rather it was said: knowledge about the spiritual world is simply not attainable; it *can* only be an object of faith.

In order to shed some light on this fact, let us look back to the times when Grecian wisdom had to retreat before a Christianized Rome. When the last Grecian philosophy schools were closed by the Emperor Justinian, the last keepers of the old wisdom migrated out of the region where European spirituality was meant to develop. They found a home in the Gondishapur Academy in Asia. This was one of the places in the east where, through Alexander's actions, the old knowledge was preserved in the form Aristotle had been able to give it.

But it was then taken over by the oriental stream which could be called Arabism. On the one hand, Arabism was a premature unfolding of the Consciousness Soul. It offered the possibility of a premature soul-life working in the direction of the Consciousness Soul to spread like a spiritual wave from Asia to Africa and southern and western Europe, and filled certain Europeans with an intellectualism which should only have appeared later on. In the seventh and eighth centuries southern and western Europe received spiritual impulses which should not have appeared before the Consciousness Soul epoch. That spiritual wave could awaken the intellectual in man; not, however, the more profound experience through which the soul enters into the spirit-world.

Although the human being activated his intellectual ability from the fifteenth to the nineteenth centuries, he could only reach a profundity of soul which did not touch the spiritual world. The Arabism which entered into European spiritual life held man's intellect back from the spirit-world. It brought the intellect — prematurely — into an activity that could only grasp the natural world.

And this Arabism proved itself to be very powerful. Whoever absorbed it began to feel — mostly unconsciously — pride in his soul. He felt the power of intellectualism; but not the incapability of the *mere* intellect to penetrate reality. Thus he gave himself over to the external reality of the senses, but it did not occur to him to approach spiritual reality.

This was the case for spiritual life during the middle ages. It had the vast traditions of the spirit-world; but the mind was so intellectually impregnated — one might even say secretly — by Arabism, that knowledge had no access to the sources from which these traditions derived.

From the early middle ages on, a battle went on between what man felt instinctively as a relation to the spirit, and the form thinking had absorbed through Arabism. One felt the world of ideas within. He experienced it as something real. But he didn't find the strength in his soul to experience the spirit in the ideas. Thus *realism* arose, which felt that reality existed in the ideas, but could not find this reality. Realism heard the cosmic word speaking in the world of ideas, but was incapable of understanding its language.

Nominalism, opposed to this view, denied that the speaking even existed because it could not be understood. According to nominalism, the world of ideas was only a sum of formulas in the human mind without roots in a spiritual reality.

This current continued into the nineteenth century. *Nominalism* became the mode of thinking for knowledge of nature. It constructed a magnificent system for the observation of the natural world, but destroyed insight into the essence of the world of ideas. *Realism* experienced a lifeless existence. It knew about the reality of the world of ideas, but could not attain to it with living knowledge.

We will attain to it when Anthroposophy finds the way from the ideas to the spiritual experience *in the ideas*. Truly progressive realism, as a path of knowledge, must stand side by side with natural scientific nominalism, thereby showing that knowledge of the spiritual in humanity is not extinguished, but can be renewed in human evolution by newly opened sources in the soul.

Goetheanum, March 1925

177. Observing the development of humanity in the natural-scientific age initially offers a sad perspective. Human knowledge with respect to the outer world is brilliant. One the other hand, a kind of consciousness has arisen which considers that knowledge of the spirit-world is no longer even possible.

178. It *seems* as though man possessed *such* knowledge only in ancient times and that as regards the spiritual world one must be satisfied accepting the old traditions and making them objects of faith.

179. Due to the resulting uncertainty in respect to the relation of man to the spiritual world during the middle ages, a disbelief in the spiritual content of ideas arose in *nominalism*, the continuation of which is the modern view of nature; and as the awareness of the reality of ideas in *realism* which, however, can only find its realization through Anthroposophy.

The Historical Turbulence at the Dawning of the Consciousness Soul

The downfall of the Roman Empire in conjunction with the appearance of peoples who arrived from the east — the so-called migration of nations — is a historical event which the researcher must always keep in mind. For the present still contains many aftereffects of these historical shocks. But an understanding of these events is not available to external historical considerations. One must look into the souls of the people involved in the "migration of nations" and the downfall of the Roman Empire.

The Greek and Roman cultures blossomed during the unfolding of the Comprehension or Sensitivity Soul. Yes, the Greeks and the Romans were the essential bearers of this unfolding. But the development of this stage in those peoples did not contain a seed which would allow the Consciousness Soul to develop in the right way *from itself.* All the spirit and soul contents in the Comprehension or Sensitivity Soul came to light in the rich life of Greek and Roman culture. It could not however advance under its own power to the Consciousness Soul.

Nevertheless, the Consciousness Soul stage did appear of course. It was as if the Consciousness Soul did not emerge from the personality of the Greek and the Roman, but from something implanted from outside.

The bonding and the release from the divine-spiritual essence, about which so much has been said in these considerations, occurs in the course of time with differing intensity. In ancient times it occurred in human evolution as a powerful intervention. During the first Christian century in Greece and Rome its power was weaker, but it did exist. As long as the Comprehension or Sensitivity Soul unfolded in them, the Greek and the Roman felt — unconsciously, but meaningfully for the soul — release from the divine-spiritual essence, along with increasing human independence. This ceased in the first Christian centuries. The dawning of the Consciousness Soul was experienced as a renewed connectedness to the divine-spiritual. Evolution was reversed from a greater to a lesser independence of soul. Christian content could not be integrated in the human Consciousness Soul because the latter could not yet be integrated into humanity.

Therefore Christian content was experienced as something given from without, from the spiritual exterior world, but not something with which one could conjoin by means of one's own knowledge.

It was otherwise with the peoples who came from the Northeast. They went through the Comprehension or Sensitivity Soul stage in a way which they felt was dependent on the spirit-world. They began to feel a degree of human independence when the earliest forces of the Consciousness Soul dawned at the beginnings of Christianity. For them the Consciousness Soul was directly bound to humanity. They felt a pious inner unfolding of forces as the Consciousness Soul awoke in them.

In this sprouting dawn of the Consciousness Soul those peoples received Christianity. They felt it as something born in their souls, not as something given from without.

This was the attitude with which those peoples approached the Roman Empire and all its attributes. It was the attitude of Arianism [*the doctrines of Arius, denying that Jesus was of the same substance as God and holding instead that he was only the highest of created beings, viewed as heretical by most Christian churches*] as opposed to athanasianism [*the teachings of Athanasius, 4th-century bishop of Alexandria, asserting that Christ is of the same substance as God; adopted by the Council of Nicaea as orthodox doctrine*]. A profound antithesis in world history.

At first only the in-streaming divine-spiritual essence acted in the Roman and the Greek Consciousness Soul — still external to humanity; it was not yet fully united with their earthly life. In the dawning Consciousness Soul of the Franks, Germans and so forth, the unification of the divine-spiritual with humanity was still *weak*.

Then the Christian content — which lived in the Consciousness Soul that hovered over humanity — began to spread, but it remained an inner urge, an impulse within humanity awaiting its unfolding, which can occur only when a certain stage in the unfolding of the Consciousness Soul has been reached.

The time beginning with the first Christian centuries until the Consciousness Soul age was one in which man could not unite knowledge with spiritual content. Therefore he connected externally to it. He "explained" it and thought about why soul forces were not sufficient to achieve cognitive union with it. He differentiated between the areas where knowledge was sufficient and those where it was not. He renounced activating soul forces to obtain knowledge of the spirit-world. And then came the time at the turn of seventeenth and eighteenth centuries when the soul forces which were inclined towards spiritual knowledge were completely diverted from it. Man began to live exclusively in the soul forces which were directed towards sense perception. The forces for knowledge of the spirit became apathetic, especially during the eighteenth century.

Thinkers lost the spiritual content in their ideas. In the idealism of the first half of the nineteenth century they presented spiritless ideas as the creative world content — Fichte, Schelling, Hegel, for example; or they pointed to something super-sensible which evaporates because it is bereft of spirit — Spencer, John Stuart Mill and others. Ideas are dead when they do not seek the living spirit. The spiritual vision for the spiritual was now lost.

A "continuation" of the old spiritual knowledge is not possible. The human soul forces, with the Consciousness Soul unfolding in them, must strive for a renewed elementary and directly living union with the spirit-world. Anthroposophy wishes to be this striving.

In the spiritual/cultural life of the present age, it is first and foremost the leading personalities who do not know what Anthroposophy wants to do. And therefore many others who follow them are also deterred. The leaders live in a soul content which has gradually become unaccustomed to using spiritual forces. For them it is as though a person with a paralyzed organ were called upon to use it. For in the time from the sixteenth century till the second half of the nineteenth century the higher forces of knowledge were paralyzed. And humanity was completely unconscious of this; it considered the one-sided use of knowledge directed to the world of the senses as great progress.

Goetheanum, March 1925

180. The Greeks and the Romans were especially predisposed for the unfolding of the Comprehension or Sensitivity Soul. They developed this soul stage to perfection. But they did not possess the inherent seeds for direct progression to the Consciousness Soul. Their soul-life stalled in the Comprehension or Sensitivity Soul stage.

181. But in the time from the rise of Christianity till the age of the Consciousness Soul evolution a spirit was at work which did not unite with human soul forces. These soul forces "explained" the spirit-world, but did not experience it.

182. The peoples who advanced with the so-called "migration of nations" from the north-east toward the Roman Empire felt within them the existence of the Comprehension or Sensitivity Soul. On the other hand, the Consciousness Soul was forming in this imbedded feeling. The inner life of those peoples was waiting for the time when the unification of the soul [mind] with the spirit-world is again possible.

From Nature to Sub-Nature

It is said that the age of philosophy was superseded by the *natural-scientific* age in the middle of the nineteenth century. And it is also said that this natural-scientific age continues still today, although many emphasize that certain philosophical intentions have been reiterated.

All this corresponds to the paths of knowledge which has been initiated in modern times, but not the *paths of life*. Man still lives in nature with his thoughts, even though he brings mechanistic thinking into his concept of nature. With his volition he lives so much in mechanical, technical processes, that it has imbued the natural-scientific age with a completely new nuance.

In order to understand human life, one must begin by considering it from two sides. From his previous earth-lives man brings his capacity to understand the cosmos acting from the periphery into the earth. He perceives with his senses what is acting on the earth from the cosmos, and through his thinking organization he thinks about the cosmos acting on the earth from the periphery. Thus through his physical body man lives in perception, through his etheric body in thinking.

What happens in his astral body and his I, works in hidden regions of his soul. It is at work, for example, in his destiny. However, one must not begin seeking it in complicated situations of destiny, but in the elementary, everyday events of life.

Man binds himself with certain earthly forces in that he orients his organism with these forces. He learns to stand upright and to walk, he learns to position himself with his arms and hands in the equilibrium of the earthly forces. *These* force are not those which stream in from the cosmos, rather are they simply earthly.

In reality nothing the human being experiences is an abstraction. He only doesn't see where the experience comes from, so he constructs abstractions from ideas about realities. He talks about mechanical laws. He thinks he has abstracted them from the world of nature. That is, however, not the case; rather all the purely mechanical laws man experiences in his soul are related to his orientation to the earth (standing, walking, etc.).

This clearly indicates that mechanics are purely earth oriented. For the laws of nature concerning color, sound and so forth have streamed to earth from the cosmos. It is only in the earthly region where the mechanical is implanted in the natural laws, as it is first implanted and experienced by the human being on earth.

Far and away the most active element that works through technology into today's civilization, and in which it is so involved, is *not nature*, but *sub-nature*. It is a world that emancipates itself downwardly from nature.

When the oriental strives for the spirit he tries to leave the equilibrium which derives from the earth. He assumes a position of meditation which brings him into cosmic equilibrium. The earth no longer affects his organism's orientation. (This is not for the purpose of imitation, but only to clarify what is meant here. Anyone familiar with my writings knows how in this respect spiritual life in the East and in the West differ.)

The human being needed this relation to the earth for the development of his Consciousness Soul. In recent times the tendency has arisen to experience in actual doing everything man needs for this development. In settling in the earthly region he encounters the Ahrimanic element. With his own resources he must find the right relation to this Ahrimanic element.

But in the technological age he has so far not been able to acquire the correct relationship to Ahrimanic civilization. Man must find the strength, the inner cognitive force in order not to be overwhelmed by Ahriman in this technological culture. Sub-nature must be understood as such. This is only possible when man reaches at least as far up in outer-earthly "supra-nature" as he has descended into technological sub-nature. The times require knowledge that transcends nature, because it must get the better of an dangerous inner life content which has descended to a level below nature.

Of course we are not suggesting that previous stages of civilization should be repeated, but that a way must be found by humanity which leads to the correct relation between the new cultural situation, himself, and the cosmos.

Nowadays only the very few realize what meaningful spiritual tasks await humanity. Electricity, which after its discovery was celebrated as the soul of nature's existence, must be recognized for its ability to divert from nature downwards to sub-nature. Man must not allow himself to be diverted along with it.

In the times when a technology independent of nature did not exist, man found the spirit *through* the observation of nature. Technology made independent of nature caused humanity to concentrate on mechanistic materiality as the only reliable science. In this all the divine-spiritual essence related to the genesis of human evolution is absent. This sphere of activity is dominated by the Ahrimanic.

In spiritual science the other sphere is created in which the Ahrimanic is not present. And it is just in the cognitive absorption of that spirituality, to which the Ahrimanic has no access, where humanity is strengthened in order to confront Ahriman *in the world*.

Goetheanum, March 1925

183. In the natural scientific age, which began in the middle of the nineteenth century, the cultural activities of humanity have been gradually sliding down not only to nature's lowest regions, but *under* nature. Technology has become sub-nature.

184. This demands that man find a spiritual cognition in which he raises himself as far into supra-nature as he has sunk under nature with sub-natural technological activity. Thereby he creates the inner strength *not* to go under.

185. An earlier conception of nature still contained the spirit, with which the source of human evolution is united; gradually this spirit has disappeared from the conception of nature and has been replaced by purely Ahrimanic concepts that have passed over into what is a technological civilization [culture].

Rudolf Steiner died on March 30,1925. These are the last words he wrote. At the time radios were still a rarity, it was still the age of steamboats and books were set by hand. Technology and electronics were in their infancy. (Trans.)

About The Translator

Frank Thomas Smith is an American expatriate originally from Brooklyn, New York. Working in the international airline business, he has lived most of his life abroad, in Europe and South America. He has moonlighted in consulting, education (Waldorf) and writing. He is the editor and publisher of the on-line e.Zine, Southern Cross Review: https://SouthernCrossReview.org/

Contact: fts@SouthernCrossReview.org

ON-LINE ACTIVITIES

What is Anthroposophy?

Rudolf Steiner described Anthroposophy as a path of knowledge to guide the spiritual in the human being to the spiritual in the cosmos. It manifests as a necessity of the heart and feeling. It is for those who feel that certain questions about the nature of man and the world are basic necessities of life, like hunger and thirst. He was a clairvoyant who spoke from his direct cognition of the spiritual world. However, he did not see his work as a religion or as sectarian, but rather sought to found a universal 'science of the spirit.' A fundamental aspect of Anthroposophy is the recognition of a real spiritual world in addition to the visible physical one.

All of Rudolf Steiner's books and thousands of lectures which have been translated into English are available free of charge at the Rudolf Steiner e.Lib.

Visit the author's e.Zine, www.SouthernCrossReview.org

Visit other versions of this work, go.elib.com/GA026.

Visit the Rudolf Steiner e.Lib, www.RudolfSteinereLib.org.

Other Books

authored or translated by
Frank Thomas Smith
All titles available at Amazon.com

ANTHROPOSOPHICAL FANTASIES (by Roberto Fox, as told to Frank Thomas Smith): Anthroposophy, also known as Spiritual Science, is not known for fantastic literature, or fiction at all. So how can stories with titles like "Life on Mars," or "The Girl in the Floppy Hat," or "To Hunt a Nazi" qualify as anthroposophical. They do not — until now. Therefore, this book is groundbreaking. You may smile at times, even laugh; other stories may cause a lump in your throat ...

ISBN: 978-1-948302-10-4

CORONAVIRUS PANDEMIC II (by Judith von Halle, translated by Frank Thomas Smith): In this book, the main focus is not on the distressing social developments that have arisen as consequence of the coronavirus pandemic – and for good reason: Although there are already (thankfully) many quality descriptions and articles about this complex of problems and questions, at the same time on the other hand a dangerous knowledge-vacuum has arisen. Therefore in this book I will refrain from elaborating on the problems already made widely visible in favor of this knowledge-vacuum, which will be outlined as an addition to what has already been described in Vol. I.

ISBN: 978-1-948302-35-7

ESOTERIC LESSONS FOR THE FIRST CLASS Volumes I, II, and III (Rudolf Steiner, translated by Frank Thomas Smith): During the re-founding of the Anthroposophical Society at Christmas 1923, Rudolf Steiner also reconstituted the 'Esoteric School' which had originally functioned in Germany from 1904 until 1914, when the outset of the First World War made it's continuance impossible. Twenty-eight lectures in three Volumes with in-line illustrations and blackboard drawings.

**ISBN: 978-1-948302-28-9 (vol. 1),
978-1-948302-30-2 (vol. 2),
978-1-948302-33-3 (vol. 3).**

FAVELA CHILDREN (by Ute Craemer, translated by Frank Thomas Smith): Ute Craemer is an educator and social worker who has dedicated over fifty years of her life to teaching and nurturing the poor children of the favelas (slums) in Brazil. As an experienced Waldorf teacher, she has been able to understand the needs of the children and their families and provide them with the spiritual nourishment they cry out for. Favela Children is a moving and informative account of Ute's Craemer's social work in the favelas and of her personal development ...

ISBN: 978-1-948302-42-5

THE HISTORY AND ACTUALITY OF IMPERIALISM (Rudolf Steiner, translated by Frank Thomas Smith): In 1920 Rudolf Steiner had already foreseen that the future imperialism would be economic rather than military or nationalistic. In these three lectures he describes the history of imperialism from ancient times to the present and into the future. The Anglo-American would play an increasingly important role in future developments, so the English visitors who attended must have been especially attentive.

ISBN: 978-1-948302-20-3

TOWARD A THREEFOLD SOCIETY (Rudolf Steiner, translated by Frank Thomas Smith): This work, written late in the life of Rudolf Steiner, makes use of a threefold analysis of the human individual and of human society. Man as an individual, or in a group, functions basically in three modes: thinking/perceiving, feeling/valuing, and willing/planning/acting. A unit of functioning, whether a part of an individual or part of a society has its proper role. Each role needs a certain respect from other areas if it is to function properly ...

ISBN: 978-1-948302-16-6

Printed in the USA
CPSIA information can be obtained
at www.ICGtesting.com
CBHW072034300624
10829CB00023B/124

9 781948 302418